Hitler
and
Mussolini
The Wester...

KU-083-908

Margaret A Pullar Smith

CONTRASTS
IN
HISTORY

Blackie

GENERAL EDITOR:
Duncan MacIntyre
Senior Lecturer in History
Jordanhill College of Education
Glasgow

For S.P.S. and M.M.S.

ISBN 0 216 90382 3

PUBLISHED BY:
Blackie & Son Limited
Bishopbriggs, Glasgow G64 2NZ
450 Edgware Road, London W2 1EG

PRINTED IN GREAT BRITAIN BY:
Robert MacLehose & Co. Ltd, Glasgow

General Editor's Preface

Contrasts in History is designed for use by students preparing for G.C.E. O Level and S.C.E. O Grade examinations. The volumes in the series could also be used for work of a more advanced nature.

Although the need to provide a narrative framework is not overlooked, the real intention is that each volume, by identifying and analysing problems, should introduce readers to the complexities of historical personalities and situations.

It is hoped that a series which illustrates the many-sided nature of events and periods, examines contrasts within and between societies, demonstrates the interplay of change and continuity, and seeks to create an awareness of differing interpretations, will help to build up a sense of the past and encourage the development of thinking skills.

DUNCAN MACINTYRE

Acknowledgments

The author and publisher wish to thank the following for permission to reproduce the photographs listed below.

Keystone Press Agency: *page 19*
Institute of Contemporary History and Wiener Library: *pages 33, 36, 44, 56 (left)*
Ullstein Bilderdienst: *pages 43, 60 (foot)*
Prentice-Hall Inc.: *page 56 (right)*
Cartoon by David Low by arrangement with the Trustees and the London *Evening Standard*: *page 57*
Herbert Block ("Herblock") and *The Washington Post*: *page 58*
Bildarchiv Preussischer Kulturbesitz: *pages 59, 60 (top)*
Popperfoto: *page 61 (top)*
The Mansell Collection: *page 61 (foot)*

Contents

1

Before the Dictators

The making of Italy and Germany took place at much the same time. In both countries unification was achieved more by force and forceful personalities than by the will of the people. In each case the state most involved in the movement for unification provided the new kingdom with its monarch. Victor Emmanuel II, King of Piedmont, was recognized as King of Italy in 1861, Wilhelm I of Prussia was proclaimed German Emperor in 1871. In each case the main architect of unity became the new kingdom's chief minister. Camillo Cavour, Piedmont's Prime Minister, became Prime Minister of Italy, and Otto von Bismarck, Prussian Chancellor, took office as German Chancellor. However, despite apparent similarities, there were important differences which were to have far reaching effects.

Italian unification was the ambition of a small, predominantly middle-class minority. It was only finally achieved with foreign help. By 1861 most of Italy was united, with Victor Emmanuel as its king. When Cavour died in that year, his last words were: "*Italy is made. All is safe.*" He was wrong. Venice and Rome were still not part of Italy and without them, Italy was not "made". Many serious problems faced the Government in trying to fuse the different states, with their different traditions and outlooks, into one state, so all was not safe. The making of Italy still had to be completed and the making of Italians begun.

The Austro-Prussian War of 1866 gave Venice back to Italy. In return for supporting Prussia against Austria, Italy was promised Venice. The war was over quickly and victoriously for Prussia, who defeated Austria decisively at Sadowa, though Italian forces, defeated by land and sea, were less successful. The armistice which followed Sadowa was drawn up without consulting Italy and the terms of the peace treaty were such that Venice was given to France, who then gave it to Italy. This important step towards Italy's unification was completed therefore not by Italian victory, but by a humiliating "hand-out" from a foreign power not directly involved in the war. This, added to

ITALY 1861

the failure of Italian forces, led to a military inferiority complex which
was to have serious consequences.

Only Rome now remained. As the ancient centre of the Roman
Empire, it was essential to Italy for reasons of prestige. It was now the
last stronghold of the temporal power of the Papacy, and as such, was of
interest to Catholic powers outside Italy. Napoleon III of France had
long felt it France's duty to protect the Pope and Papal territory from
Italy. The Empress Eugenie said firmly:

Better the Prussians in Paris than the Italians in Rome.[1]

By 1871 both had come about.

In 1870, France was manipulated into war with Prussia. After
early Prussian successes, the French garrison was withdrawn from
Rome. Defending France had become more important than protecting
the Papacy. Without foreign help, Rome lay at the mercy of Victor
Emmanuel's forces. Since Pope Pius IX refused to come to terms
peacefully, Rome was occupied and became the capital of a united

Italy. The Italian Government, not wanting to offend Catholics in and out of Italy, made it clear that the taking of Rome did not mean the enslavement of the Church. By a law of 1870, papal sovereignty was recognized within the Vatican and a large sum of money offered in lieu of territories lost by the Papacy. The Pope refused to recognize the law and thus set the pattern of papal attitudes to Italian governments for many years. (It was not till 1929 that agreement was finally reached.)

The papal declaration of its infallibility (1870) was, in Italy, backed up by an order forbidding Catholics to take any part in government, either as voters or as deputies. This was to have a serious effect on Italian public life in general and politics in particular as it restricted political development and kept many able men out of political life. It was not till just before the First World War that the papal order was more and more ignored. The embargo had the effect too of widening the existing gap between the people and their government. As unification had not been the will of the majority, the gap was inevitable. The fact that the minority in favour of unification had only achieved it with foreign help, made it wider and did little to add to respect for government. And the form that government took did not help.

Italy had a typical nineteenth-century liberal constitution. The King was head of State, with some executive and legislative powers. Ministers were responsible to him, though gradually in Italy, ministers became more and more responsible to Parliament. The King also nominated members of the Senate or Upper House. The Chamber of Deputies, or Lower House, was an elected body but the narrow property franchise took away much of its "representative" aspect. In 1871 only 1·98 per cent of Italians had the vote. The papal ruling, obeyed by most devout Catholics, coupled with this limited franchise, meant that Italy had no truly representative government. A genuine political contest was almost unknown in the constituencies. It was usual for the most powerful local man or his nominee to be chosen who, once in Parliament, was unwilling to leave. As a result, oligarchic, not democratic, rule developed. The parties themselves had similar policies and thus clearly defined and effective party politics was almost un-known in Italy. Between 1860 and 1922 there were thirty-eight govern-ments, as well as much cabinet shuffling, but still no positive policy emerged. Because of the number of parties and this lack of clear-cut policies it was impossible to build up a sufficiently stable majority in Parliament to give reliable support to any government. The remedy for this was to develop party managers who could arrange a majority. This led, inevitably, to bribery, corruption and scandals. Many Italians grew more and more distrustful of politics and politicians, and became indifferent to a regime they could neither share in nor respect.

Putting unification into practice brought many problems. Money, which Italy could ill afford after the initial cost of unification, had to be spent in providing uniformity in the armed forces, the judiciary and the Civil Service. Communications had to be provided to unite the country physically. People had to be encouraged to consider themselves Italian, not Piedmontese, Tuscan or Sicilian. Superimposed on all this was the basic "north and south" problem. Farming was the main occupation of the Italians. Most of the farmers were peasant farmers, working the land for big landlords. Only in the north were there any industrial towns. The south was poor, barren and lawless and had not been enthusiastic for unification. It was a foreign country to the northerners, who saw it as a barrier to progress. The north had more fertile land, industry and more influence in Rome. As a result, little was done to solve the problems of the south. Repression rather than help was the policy.

The growing industrialization was becoming a problem. Initially, the landlords who formed the main part of the governing class took little interest in home industry. It was foreign investment which started up heavy industry in Italy and it was not till the twentieth century that the Italians themselves began to take a large part in the industrial growth of their country by investing heavily and becoming involved in the development. Without government control, the bigger companies took over smaller ones, and by 1914, Italian industry was controlled by a small group who ran it to suit themselves and their profits.

The growth of industry drew people to the towns of the north and urban poverty became another problem. The workers were exploited by the industrialists and not protected by the Government. Strikes and rural disturbances were put down with equal severity and little investigation into their cause. In this situation, the Socialist movement, based on the teachings of Karl Marx, grew, and the Socialist party began to play a part in politics. In the years before the First World War, Catholics in Italy began to take a greater interest in public life and to enter politics, despite the papal ban. They represented the Right as the Socialists represented the Left. After a series of constitutional crises in the early years of the twentieth century, brought about by attempts to give Italy a more positive government, some changes were made. The man who dominated politics between 1903 and 1914 was Giovanni Giolitti. He was the last and greatest of the political managers. He determined to stay in power at all costs and played the Right off against the Left to do this. There were electoral changes, and the introduction of universal male suffrage in 1912 gave the vote to many more people. However, a large proportion of the eight million now enfranchised were still illiterate, so local influence still affected the outcome of elections in many constituencies.

The growth of heavy industry meant the need for a source of raw materials and an outlet for manufactured goods. Italy had lost out in the scramble for Africa in the early stages and her attempt to conquer Abyssinia in 1896 ended in defeat at Adowa. An articulate nationalist movement had developed which aimed at giving Italy prestige by overseas possessions and this, coupled with the self-interest of the industrialists, led to Italy becoming involved in war with Turkey in 1912. Success in this war brought her Libya, but it was a costly venture and Libya proved to be useful neither as a source of raw materials, nor as an outlet for goods.

In the months leading up to the start of the First World War, Italy faced serious economic and constitutional problems. This led to strikes and angry demonstrations, as the slump following the Libyan campaign caused cuts in wages and unemployment for many. However, despite a Socialist threat, law and order were restored. The outbreak of war presented another problem that was to lead to a long and bitter debate—whether to join in or stay neutral. Italy was officially the ally of Austria and Germany. It had not been a popular alliance with the majority of Italians, and German arrogance and condescension had made matters worse. Many, in particular the Nationalists, disliked an alliance with a country like Austria, which had stood for so long in the path of Italian unification. The King, the Nationalists and the business sector, seeing profit in war, were in favour of intervention. The Socialists and most of the Government felt intervention would bring nothing but trouble. With the Socialists it was a matter of principle; with the Government, one of cost. They felt too that Italy would gain as much from bribes to stay out as she would from promises of help if she joined in, but it was clear that intervention, if it came, would be on the Anglo-French side. If France were defeated, nothing would stand between Italy and a German-Austrian take-over. In the debate the pro-war group got their way. The King and the Prime Minister of the time, Antonio Salandra, kept secret their private negotiations with the Allies, which bound Italy to join the war on the Anglo-French side.

The war went badly for Italy. Conditions at the Front were appalling. The army lacked up-to-date equipment and good leaders.

Most of the men were illiterate peasants who had no idea what the war was about. They had joined up, believing the promises of the politicians that victory would bring them justice and ownership of their land. The army was defeated at Caporetto in 1917, and though it gained a victory at Vittorio Veneto in 1918, this was with allied help.

Soldiers at the Front did gain in one respect. They were able to talk together and air grievances about their lot. This, and a sharing in suffering, gave them a feeling of unity. At home, war brought a boom in industry, full employment and rising wages. The rise in the cost of living was hardly noticed and the speculators and industrialists made fortunes. Soldiers on leave felt very bitter about it, and having to suffer the taunts of the Socialists about fighting in a war that was not *their* affair made matters worse. In politics too the interventionist debate went on. Italy's failure to win glory gave each side a grievance. When

THE ITALIAN FRONT

peace came, the Government was as weak as it had ever been. Their position grew worse when the terms of the peace settlement were known. With the war over, Italy's usefulness as an ally was over. Her contribution did not give her a large say in the talks. She did not even get the territory promised in 1915; Signor Orlando called it a "mutilated victory". The interventionists felt cheated. The neutralists felt betrayed.

Post-war elections in 1919 returned a Parliament in which two parties had the chance of positive action. The Socialists had 156 seats and the Popolari (Catholic) party had 100. Though neither had an overall majority, they could have governed in a coalition. However, both parties were split internally and too far apart ideologically to do anything, and because between them they held over half the seats in Parliament, they also prevented anyone else from trying.

Parliament, unable to form a durable, effective government, had to face the post-war problems of unemployment and depression and the threat of revolution. There were fewer jobs, wages fell, and the cost of living rose. Ex-servicemen coming home were bitter to find the promises made to them could not be kept. This was the situation in Italy in 1919, when Benito Mussolini formed his Fascist party.

Germany's unification, unlike that of Italy, owed nothing to foreign aid. Nor was there a problem like that of the Papacy to complicate the matter and give foreign powers an excuse for interference. Unification came about as the result of Bismarck's efforts to assert Prussian supremacy in the German states. Otto von Bismarck, a Junker politician, became Chancellor of Prussia in 1862 as the result of a constitutional crisis. By 1871 he had transformed Prussia into a great power and the Prussian King into German Emperor. He had little time for parliamentary regimes or liberal politicians. In his view:
> The great questions of the day will not be settled by resolutions and majority votes . . . but by blood and iron.[2]

Bismarck never aimed at a unification of Germany that would include Austria. He wanted leadership for Prussia and blocked any attempt by Austria to get unification by general agreement among the German states. He was a realist in every way, as his reply to his fiancée's comment on loyalty shows:
> By the way, the sentence "loyalty is the very fire that forever vivifies and sustains the heart of existence" is one of those nebulous, misty phrases from which it is difficult to derive any clear meaning and which, not infrequently, have injurious results when they are carried over from poetry to reality.[3]

7

Three short, well-conducted wars played a part in convincing the other German states to accept Prussia's leadership. War with Denmark over the provinces of Schleswig and Holstein ended in Prussian victory in 1864. Rivalry with Austria over these duchies provided the occasion for a war which Bismarck planned would dispose of Austria as a contender for leadership of a united Germany. In 1866, in a seven weeks war, Prussia defeated Austria at Sadowa, and though this defeat was not followed up, Austrian power did not recover. As far as the German states were concerned Prussia was supreme. There remained Europe. In 1870 France floundered into war with Prussia and was defeated at Sedan and Metz. Napoleon III abdicated, a republic was declared and France's position as a power in Europe received a set-back. The balance of power was completely altered.

The German princes were persuaded to offer Wilhelm I the German crown. The new German Empire, the Second Reich, was proclaimed in the Hall of Mirrors at Versailles in 1871. Unification had been achieved, with Prussia as the dominant power. It was a triumph of will rather than superiority. Prussia had neither superior men nor weapons. She was just better at exploiting her resources.

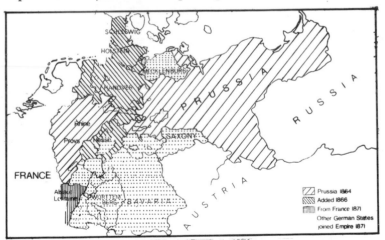

The German Empire in 1871

The next task was to build on the foundations laid. This was not easy. The princes were reluctant to accept Prussia as leader in a united Germany and many of the people felt the same way. One Prussian soldier at Versailles in 1871, said:

They hate us, these . . . Hanoverians, Bavarians, Saxons . . . they hate the very name because we have made them a nation.[4]

The only point that the princes, Bismarck and the Emperor had in common was a dislike of liberal politicians. Self-preservation was the keynote, and the new constitution was shaped to suit. Outwardly it was democratic, effectively it was autocratic. The King was head of State and Commander-in-Chief. In practice he delegated his authority to the Chancellor and the Chief of General Staff. The Upper House was made up of princes of the various component states of Germany, with Prussia as the dominant influence. The Lower House or Reichstag was elected by universal suffrage, but as it was given little power, this seeming concession to the "liberals" was hollow. Ministers were not responsible to it, but they used it to ratify their measures. As a result it was virtually impossible for political parties to develop any sense of national responsibility or to learn how to govern.

The two parties which provided what opposition there was to the Government were looked on with mistrust by both Government ministers and the country. The Social Democrats, as followers of Marx, were regarded either as traitors or "vagabonds without a Fatherland", a dig at the supra-national character of Socialism. The Centre or Catholic party was suspected of being open to papal influence and in an aggressively Protestant regime, this was regarded as dangerous. With opposition to the Government regarded as treason the normal cut and thrust of party politics could not develop.

Without real power, the Reichstag failed to attract men of ability and ambition. The road to power lay elsewhere. Sombert, the historian, put it this way:

With us (Germans), there is no diversion of talent into politics. Neither the rich, nor, what is more important, the gifted members of the middle class are withdrawn from economic life to devote themselves to politics.[2]

Politics was left as the preserve of the less able or extremists, and government in the hands of the traditional governing class. The upper and middle classes turned to industry instead of politics and used it as a substitute route to power. They concentrated on developing industries which would enhance Germany's chances of becoming a world power, supreme in Europe. To many of the middle class, involved in this way, money became equated with power. Respect and support would therefore be given to the regime which would ensure the maintenance of stable conditions for profit.

Unification brought a programme of reform. Uniformity of the coinage, the administration, the legal system and education was developed. Restrictions were removed on trade union formation and freedom of enterprise. This took away a large part of the liberal platform and social reforms like old age pensions and sickness benefit spiked the guns of Socialist attack. They also helped to make industrial trouble less likely to hamper Germany's industrial development. Bismarck put it this way:

Whoever has a pension for his old age, is far more content and far easier to handle than one who has no such prospect.

However, Germany was to find it was not as simple as that. Socialism grew and though many in the Socialist party mellowed with the security and growing industrial prosperity, the extremists were less content. While in other countries, like Britain, Socialists were beginning to take part in government and to develop in a responsible way, in Germany they were held down. The years from 1900 to 1914 saw an increasing unrest among politically-minded workers. The middle classes, fearing a financial upset, were increasingly hostile to the Socialists. Many hoped that reform could come without revolution, but feared it would not. Others, who were discontented with conditions, emigrated to America.

The war was greeted in Germany with patriotic fervour. The Kaiser, Wilhelm II, spoke to the Reichstag, calling for unity and saying:

Henceforth I know no parties, only Germans.[5]

The Socialists, against war in principle as much as the Italian Socialists had been, found their heads ruled by their hearts and voted for war. They hoped that as a result of the war there might be an extension of parliamentary participation in government. They were disappointed. The High Command took control. Even the Kaiser, addicted to the army, complained:

If the German people think I am Supreme Commander, they are grossly mistaken. The General Staff tells me nothing and never asks my advice. . . .[5]

After initial successes the war developed into stalemate, but in the late summer of 1918 the German line broke under Allied pressure. It became clear to the High Command that victory for Germany was impossible. Anxious to avoid total defeat and occupation of German soil, they were keen to ask for an armistice. The Kaiser was forced to do what politicians had wanted him to do for years, form a democratic government. A cabinet was appointed under Prince Max of Baden, who was responsible to the Reichstag. The army had kept itself and its reputation intact. The politicians so long kept out of power were to be involved in the dealings for peace. However, the Allies refused to treat with Germany as long as the Kaiser remained. Germany was war-weary and in the uncertainty following the shock of defeat, revolt and civil disorders were rife. The fleet mutinied at Kiel, and across Germany, workers' "soviets", on the lines of the Russian ones, were set up in the main towns. Extreme Socialists and Communists tried to turn the situation to their advantage and stage a real revolution.

The Kaiser abdicated and a republic was proclaimed. As the largest party in the Reichstag, the Social Democrats formed a government, led by Friedrich Ebert. The revolution and the republic were imposed on Germany more by outside interests than the carefully planned programme of any party. The Social Democrats, split and unready for responsibility, were pitchforked into action. Their extreme left wing, the Spartacists, wanted revolution and total change. The majority of the party wanted change but not revolution. The problems the Government faced were many—defeat, uncertainty of peace terms, some two million war dead, widows and orphans in great numbers to be cared for, a starving and bitter population, a ruined economy and revolts. Ebert saw his first task as the restoration of order. He accepted the help of the army to do this and the Prussian war ministry paid the volunteers who, serving under Imperial officers, made up the Frei Korps. With their help the revolution was crushed and this gave the army a stake in the future of Germany. General Groener, speaking for the High Command, put it this way:

We hoped through our action to gain a share of power in the new state for the army and the officer corps. If we succeeded, then we should have rescued for the new Germany, the best and strongest elements of the old Prussia, despite the revolution.[6] (Note the use of the word Prussia.)

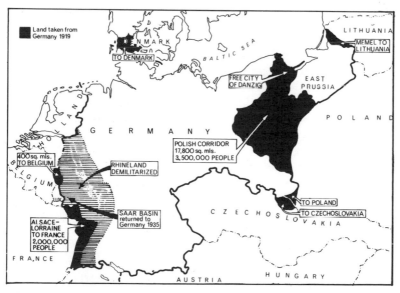

Ebert also made use of the Civil Service to get things back to normal, explaining:

We had to make sure, once we had taken over power, that the Reich machine did not break down . . . we therefore urgently appealed to all Reich officials to continue to exercise their duty till further notice.[6]

Elections for the new Assembly were held in January 1919 and once elected, it met at Weimar which was thought to be safer than Berlin. The new republic took its name from the town. The Social Democrats, though the largest party, did not have an overall majority, so they had to rely on a coalition with other parties to carry on government. The new constitution provided for a President, elected every seven years; a Reichsrat, representing the interests of the various states; and a Reichstag, elected every four years by universal suffrage. The Chancellor was appointed by the President, but was responsible to the Reichstag. Article 48 of the constitution allowed rule by decree in times of national crisis. By comparison with the old constitution, the Weimar one was almost too democratic for a Reichstag and people unused to governing and to thinking responsibly about government. The old self-interest attitude of so many parties, which in the past had merely damaged their image, could now damage the republic. Neither the republic nor the constitution satisfied any one party completely. Many felt that it was at best a compromise, at worst an interregnum. With this attitude, it is hard to see how loyalty could develop. Fritz Meinecke wrote:

Looking to the past, I remain a monarchist at heart: looking to the future, I shall become a republican by conviction. . . . The republic is the form of government that divides us least.[6]

The greatest problem for the new rulers to face was the peace treaty. Having got rid of the Kaiser, whom many felt was responsible for the war, and having changed their form of government, they hoped for generous terms. They hoped too for a negotiated peace; they got a dictated one and in their bitterness forgot about the harsh terms imposed on Russia in 1917. If the defeat of the army in 1918 shocked Germany, the Treaty of Versailles humiliated her. She had been expecting to give up some territory, but had hoped to have Austria join her in a greater Germany, not wanted by Bismarck, but the aim of many Germans. She had expected to make some reparation but nothing like the sum named. If the politicians hoped for the best and prepared for the worst, the man in the street did not. Most Germans did not realize the changed state of the world, nor Germany's position in it. They indulged in an orgy of self-pity and refused to listen to reason or to face reality. The whole balance of power had now changed and this was bound to affect the attitudes of the victors. The Russian Empire, the Habsburg Empire, the Ottoman Empire as well as the German Empire had now gone. In their place were many new, smaller states. France demanded terms which would give her security. America, whose president, Woodrow Wilson, had influenced the drawing up of the treaty, had withdrawn into isolation from European politics. Faced with trying to re-draw the map of Europe, it was unlikely that German and Allied views of what was fair would coincide. What was more important was not whether it was fair or unfair, but how the German people viewed it and how this would affect the future of the republic. Many of the criticisms of the treaty were not valid, but the German people *thought* they were, and despised a government which had signed it in the first place and was now trying to justify doing so. National pride preferred to blame Germany's failures and troubles on the Treaty of Versailles, just as military pride blamed the "November Criminals" for stabbing the army in the back and causing its defeat, rather than Allied supremacy. They refused to see that the Government had no choice but to sign. It was against this troubled background that Adolf Hitler began his rise to power with the Nazi party.

---

[1]*Risorgimento: the making of Italy* by Edgar Holt (MACMILLAN); [2]*The Course of German History* by A. J. P. Taylor (HAMISH HAMILTON, 1945); [3]*The Nazi Years* ed. by Joachim Remak (PRENTICE-HALL, 1969); [4]*Germany 1870–1970* by Roger Morgan (MACDONALD & CO., 1970); [5]*The Kaiser and his Times* by Michael Balfour (PENGUIN, 1975); [6]*From Bismarck to Hitler* by J. C. G. Roehl (BARNES & NOBLE, 1970).

2

Benito Mussolini

The inter-war years could be called the Fascist years. Fascism was active in most European countries. Those with stable governments were able to contain it. Italy and Germany were not. It was a supra-national movement, but it took different forms in different countries, so it is not easy to define. It had a basic core of violence and its great strength lay in the attraction it had for so many ordinary people, who believed in it and endorsed its·methods. Their support made it possible. A quotation from Ignazio Silone explains it this way:

You cannot have a king without subjects, or a leader without those willing to be led.[1]

Fascism in Italy was revolutionary, anti-socialist and anti-nationalist in the conservative nationalism sense, but with a nationalism of its own. Benito Mussolini, the founder of the Fascist movement in Italy defined it in this way:

The Fascist conception of the State is all-embracing; outside of it no human or spiritual values may exist, much less have any value. . . . Fascism is not only a lawgiver and a founder of institutions, but an educator . . . it enforces discipline and makes use of authority. . . . Fascism is an idea, a doctrine, a realization, is universal; it is Italian in its particular institutions, but it is universal by reason of its nature.[2]

It attracted to it many people who had no other point in common beyond being members of the party. Its violence attracted those who wanted action; its novelty attracted those disillusioned with the existing political parties. People hoped that Fascism would be able to solve Italy's problems.

Benito Mussolini was born in 1883 in Predappio, a town in the Romagna. This was an area long known for its hostility to authority. He was the son of a blacksmith and always prided himself on being a man of the people. His father was well known locally as an extreme Socialist with republican and anti-clerical views and Mussolini followed these opinions. After leaving school, he trained as a teacher, but his extreme political views made it hard for him to hold down a job for long. He went to Switzerland in 1902 and it was here that he began his career of political agitation. He lectured and wrote articles for Socialist journals. On his return to Italy he served in the army. Then he took up his career again, attacking the "establishment" and gaining a reputation in the Socialist party. He was a man of action, seeing violence rather than peaceful persuasion as a means of change. He became the leader of the extreme Socialist wing of the National Executive. His activities led to a number of spells in prison, but this, if anything, improved his standing in the party. After a further spell of teaching and some time in Austria, he became editor of *Avanti*, the leading Socialist newspaper. Through his editorials he attacked the Government, bourgeois society in general and the Nationalists. He agreed with Herve, the French Socialist, that:

the flag is a rag to be planted on a dunghill.[3]

Unrest among workers was encouraged by calls to strike. War was seen by him, as by all Socialists, as a class struggle which was no concern of Socialists in any country.

Mussolini's attempt to get into Parliament in 1912 failed, even though he stood in Forli, a place where he was well known. When war broke out in August 1914, he was one of the leading opponents of Italy's participation. His editorials were full of anti-war slogans. But by October 1914, he had changed his mind and was asking questions such as:

Do we wish, as men and Socialists, to be inert spectators of this grandiose drama? Or would we prefer to be, in some way, its protagonists?

Mussolini was obliged to resign his editorship of *Avanti* and was expelled from the Socialist party. He set up the newspaper *Il Popolo d'Italia* which advocated his personal form of militant Socialism. From being an advocate of extreme Socialism, he became in time one of its most bitter opponents and was eventually identified with the right-wing nationalist movement. After war service, during which he was wounded and invalided out, he returned to the editorship of *Il Popolo d'Italia* through which he engaged in an active campaign against the Socialist party. Again, his editorials were outspoken. He claimed, as "a man of the trenches", to speak for those fighting for Italy, who ought to have the right to rule when peace came. Once the war was over, Italy faced many problems which gave Mussolini and his followers a chance to gain favour. There were disturbances both in the countryside and in the towns. The peasants, for so long landless labourers too poor to buy their land even if the landlord would sell, took the law into their own hands. They occupied uncultivated land and organized resistance to the landlords, forming "leagues" to control power and fix wages. Violence was the rule against opposition. Fearing a revolution, many landlords sold their land and the peasants beggared themselves to buy their own holdings. As the "leagues" fixed wages to hit the pockets of the wealthier landlords, wages were too high for this new class of peasant landowners to meet. They were saddled with land they could not afford to work, and, though their own masters, were poorer than before. Peasants who had gone to work in factories during the war now found themselves unemployed and returned to the countryside. They were prepared to work for the lowest wages and were looked on by the "leagues" as blacklegs.

In the towns, workers were facing an uncertain future. They were being organized by the Socialists to strike for better conditions, higher wages and a share in the profits. The industrialists and the middle class who had invested heavily, feared revolution as much as the landowners in the countryside. The solutions offered by successive governments did little to help in the long term. It did not help either that post-war problems were worldwide. Before the war, emigration had provided an escape for discontented workers, many of whom went to America, but America had restricted her intake of immigrants, and the numbers moving to France and Britain in post-war years were not enough to take the pressure off. Violence in town and countryside grew.

Mussolini founded the Italian Fascist movement in Milan in March 1919. It began as an organization of "toughs", the Fasci di Combattimento, run on military lines, armed and wearing the black shirt. It was more concerned with action than doctrine, but what policy it had was revolutionary. At no time did Mussolini let policy stand in the way of getting valuable support. The new movement attracted few people to start with, but those who did join were dedicated men. By 1920, when unrest was growing more serious, many more became members. The Blackshirts were tough and enjoyed a fight. With their distinctive uniform, they were easily recognized by friend and foe, and in fights with the Socialists they usually won, since they were better organized and more unscrupulous. Street fights became a common sight in towns and villages, often started by the Fascists. Rather than being guardians of law and order they were as guilty as any of breaking it. However, with the help of publicity in Mussolini's journal, the message came over that the Fascists were trying to keep order, doing what the Government seemed powerless to do. He wrote:

Inside the map:

SWITZERLAND

AUSTRIA

FRANCE

TYROL····
···Conflict·
with Austria

Conflict with
Yugoslavia
Trieste
Fiume

Milan

THE
INDUSTRIAL
NORTH
Unemployment
and Strikes

ADRIATIC SEA

YUGOSLAVIA

ITALY

Rome

Sardinia

THE
AGRICULTURAL
SOUTH
Poverty and
Lawlessness

Naples

SICILY

ITALY AFTER 1918

Malta
(Br.)

The political authority was powerless; it could not control the disorders and disturbances. . . . At last, over the horizon I had brought defenders of civil life, protectors of order and citizenship. . . .[4]

What was important was that people believed what Mussolini and Fascist propaganda told them and saw them as restorers of order and protectors of property, when in reality they were just stronger and tougher.

Thus Fascism gained support from many sectors of society who thought they could use it for their own interests. Property owners and industrialists supported it to keep down strikes, squatters and Socialism. The middle class supported it because they hoped that a Fascist Italy would encourage private enterprise, defend the rights of property and protect their investments. Ex-servicemen joined it for many reasons. It promised action and violence, a continuation of the comradeship of wartime and the chance of power. Others joined it for reasons like those of Italo Balbo, who wrote:

When I returned from the war—just like so many others—I hated politics and politicians, who, in my opinion, had betrayed the hopes of the soldiers, reducing Italy to a shameful peace. . . . Mussolini gave to fighting youth that programme of radical negation of the present which they searched after . . . and even more . . . a positive mirage . . . government by youth. . . .[5]

Violence and social disorder continued, with governments doing little to control or contain it. Their attitude seemed to be summed up by Giolitti, when speaking of growing Fascist violence:

They have to give vent to their feelings.

Meanwhile, the Fascist party continued to gain strength and by 1921 had thirty-five seats in Parliament. Though it was becoming a national party its roots were regional, and in local government it exerted much influence through the "ras", the local party chiefs. Fascist activity in the regions was stepped up, with town council offices and strategic communication points being taken over, in many cases with the connivance of the local officials. By the beginning of 1922 Mussolini had a "name" in the movement and an attraction as a personality, "Il Duce". He had contacts with people in all sections of society, even the Court, despite having been anti-monarchist. He had the support of the King's younger brother, the Duke of Aosta, who hoped that a *coup* might put him on the throne. The Socialists tried to alter the course of events by calling a general strike in August. This gave Mussolini and his followers an occasion to show themselves as restorers of order and suppressors of a Socialist plot, as they were able to cause the strike to collapse while the Government stood idly by. Realizing that the time was right to assert the power of Fascism, Mussolini, addressing a Fascist rally in Naples almost 2 months later, said:

Either they will give us the government or we shall seize it by descending on Rome. It is now only a matter of days, perhaps hours. . . .

Fascist bands began to march towards the capital from various parts of Italy. They were neither as large nor as organized as people were led to believe. The ring-leaders travelled in comfort by train and waited on events. The Government, backed by the army, could have kept control if the King had declared a state of emergency, but this he refused to do. Either he felt it would be wrong on his own account or was persuaded by a pro-Fascist, possibly his brother. Instead, Mussolini was asked to come to Rome and form a government. This action took away any chance of Mussolini seizing power. He accepted the invitation, took a train to Rome and was received by the King. He came to power therefore, more by inaction on the part of the Government than direct action of his own. However, the myth of the march on Rome

This photograph shows Mussolini in morning coat, marching on Rome with his generals. Notice that the generals are all wearing black shirts with their uniform.

went into Fascist annals. Faced with the editorial choice of printing the facts or the legend, Mussolini chose the legend.

Mussolini, as Prime Minister, was now part of the establishment he had attacked for so long. Having criticized previous prime ministers and cabinets for mismanagement, he had now to justify his own position. The extremists among his followers hoped for revolutionary action, but to start with he worked within a legal framework. His first Government was a coalition, with only four of the fourteen members Fascists. Those four, however, held key posts. In addition to his post as Premier, Mussolini held the office of Foreign Minister, Minister of the Interior and President of the Council of Ministers. He explained his actions in this way:

> *I discarded the idea of a Fascist dictatorship, because I wanted to give the country the impression of normal life, far from the selfish exclusiveness of a Party. . . . I decided to compose a ministry of a Nationalist character . . . later there would become inevitable a process of clarification; but I preferred it should come . . . from the succeeding political events. . . .*[4]

Parliament gave the new government a big vote of confidence. It also gave it the right to govern by decree for one year. This in itself was not new. What was new was to give such a right to a government which could not define its policies. Mussolini did promise however that:

Constitutional liberties will not be violated; the law will be enforced at any cost.

The electoral laws were altered to ensure that the strongest party in the country got two-thirds of the seats in Parliament, while the other parties had to share the remaining third. This would make sure of a Fascist majority in Parliament. Though Mussolini was prepared to move slowly in the direction of change, his extreme followers continued their pressure and this was to cause tension in the Fascist party for the next two years. Partly to keep an eye on his rivals and also to placate them, he formed the Fascist Grand Council to advise him on government matters. One of the first things they did was to legalize the Blackshirt squads into a National Security Militia. This body swore allegiance, not to the King, but to Mussolini as his private bodyguard. This allegiance, however, did not prevent the Militia from acting against his orders and obeying local Fascist leaders. Mussolini's authority was weaker in fact than on paper.

Parliamentary support for Mussolini did not last long and even a forced amalgamation of the Nationalists with the Fascists did not give them a majority. Elections were called in 1924 with Fascist violence reaching a new peak. Violence at election time was not new in Italy, but this was a different kind of systematic violence. The Fascists gained the victory they wanted, with 65 per cent of the votes, but the violence and intimidation did not go on without protest, mainly from the Socialists; in particular their leader Matteotti. He was brutally murdered a few months later and Mussolini and the Fascists were blamed. Mussolini did not actually commit the murder, but he was responsible for it. It is said that he remarked of Matteotti:

That man ought not to be walking around.

The murder followed. It was by no means the only incident of its kind, but it was the most publicized one and Mussolini's admitted responsibility for it took away his cloak of legality. It also ruled out any chance of agreement with the Socialists. The extremists of the party were forcing Mussolini closer to dictatorship, not against his inclination but against his timing. By 1925, he was saying:

Italy wants peace and quiet, and calm to work in. This we shall give her, by love if possible, by force if need be.

Between 1925 and 1926 Mussolini's Government became exclusively Fascist. Anti-Fascist parties were banned. In the country, freely elected local councils and officials were replaced by Fascists appointed from Rome. In industry, Fascist organizations took over. Trade unions were banned. Strikes and lock-outs were forbidden. Instead, the Fascists promised better conditions for both workers and employers alike. Party members were given preference in appointments to jobs, strictly in order of seniority of service in the party. The Press fell under Fascist control, and this was a serious blow to freedom. The Italian Press had a long tradition of expressing opinions forcibly; Mussolini's years as a journalist proved that. Now there was to be censorship and Fascists in charge of the leading papers, which would become, in effect, Fascist mouthpieces. By 1926 Italy was a dictatorship, though the King and the Upper House remained. Despite earlier republican opinions Mussolini did not remove the monarchy. Nor did he do anything to destroy the Church, despite his anti-clerical views. In fact Mussolini was responsible for the agreement that was reached with the Papacy, the first since 1870. It was a big contribution to national unity. Papal fears of a Socialist take-over in Italy had led to a softening attitude by 1922 and, though officially at odds with Fascism, a *modus vivendi* had developed. There were however still those devout Catholics who remained faithful to the 1870 edict, so a real solution was important.

Fascism seemed to represent much of which the Church could approve. It was anti-Socialist, pro-national, and anti-Bolshevik. Pius XI had shown goodwill by not interfering when the Popolari party was banned along with the other political parties. Once in power, Mussolini held out an olive branch by restoring some Catholic privileges in schools and increasing the State allowance to priests. Both sides needed the other and Papal approval of the Fascists gave Mussolini a great psychological advantage. The Lateran Treaty of 1929 set the seal on this and gave the lead to many devout Catholics, both in Italy and elsewhere, to support or condone a movement which, in other circumstances, they might have condemned. Catholicism was recognized as the sole religion of the State. Church schools had equal status with State schools and religious education was compulsory in all secondary schools. The Vatican was recognized as Papal territory and compensation was paid to the Papacy for lands lost. In return, the Papacy at last recognized the Italian State.

In immediate and practical terms, the Papacy hoped that the Fascists would suppress the Socialists, keep the Bolsheviks at bay and restore law and order. But by compromising with Fascism which was anti-Christian, the Papacy weakened its position as the supra-national spokesman of Christian opposition to later Fascist (and Nazi) excesses.

Whatever effect the treaty had on the Church, however, it certainly boosted Mussolini's popularity, particularly in the less-educated but devout sections of the community. This helped to counter the ill effects of the Fascist economic policy.

In 1926, Mussolini had claimed:

We are a State which controls all forces of society. We control moral forces; we control political forces; we control economic forces, therefore we are a full-blown Corporative State.[6]

The idea behind this was to get away from divisions in society and aim at a classless state. Branches of economic activity were designated and each branch had to organize itself efficiently, with representatives from capital and labour on an equal footing. It was to be similar to the Craft Gilds of the heyday of the Middle Ages, with each craft responsible for its own organization, conditions and hours of work, disputes, training and standards. In them, master, journeyman and apprentice were merely different stages in the training programme and there was no division between employer and employee, though even in the Middle Ages this was more an ideal than a long-term reality. In twentieth-century Italy it was not a success. It involved a great deal of form-filling and bureaucracy. Some branches never got the scheme organized at all. In those where it was started there was gross inefficiency, and corruption was rife. As strikes were forbidden there was no equality in bargaining power between master and man. Exploitation and chaos resulted, and although some industrialists made big profits, economically it was a disaster. However, through the use of propaganda it did appear to some to be a success and of course Mussolini took some credit for it. His prestige was enhanced, and by ensuring that schemes like the draining of the Pontine Marshes were seen by as many people as possible, an illusion was created of a vigorous, lively economy. Areas less likely to be seen suffered from delays in plans for improvements and the usual local profiteering.

Wages fell and unemployment remained high, reaching the two million mark in 1932. The cost of living did not fall so there was a consequent drop in living and health standards. The lower classes felt the pinch first, but soon all but a small number of Italians were suffering economic hardship. Not until the years just before the outbreak of the Second World War did conditions improve and this was due to preparation for war rather than a real economic improvement.

Having established his Fascist State, Mussolini then turned his attention to involving the Italian people in it. As he had no programme to present he had to offer them what *seemed* to be a programme.

This he achieved, or tried to achieve, by propaganda. As a journalist he had used words to put over his message in editorials. As Il Duce he continued to use them, but he was well aware that words in journals and newspapers would reach only a limited number of people, many Italians being still illiterate, or semi-literate. Visual aids in the form of posters, symbols and short succinct slogans were used. Slogans like: *"Mussolini is always right"* or *"Believe, obey, fight!"* were easy to recognize, understand and remember. Symbols were important too. The Fascist symbol of the axe and lictors' rods was taken from Ancient Rome and served as an advertisement and a reminder of the Fascist State.

The Fascists also made full use of the growing wireless industry (Marconi was an Italian) and the new development in the cinema, talking pictures. They were the mass media of the time. Money was poured into both industries to help their development and at the same time speed up their use for Fascist propaganda. With films, Fascism could invade the world of entertainment; with radio, it could be in the living room of many families. Cheap cinema seats and cheap radios were extremely useful to the Fascists. Fascism could reach a wide audience in its less guarded moments, an audience bigger than any seen at rallies, and though Mussolini preferred a live audience, there were others to do the broadcasting. Strict censorship made sure that only suitable material was shown or transmitted.

Journalism operated in the same restricted way. Fascist news-papers and journals grew in number, providing jobs for party members who would never have got a job in journalism on the open market. As a result not only did truth disappear, but the standard of journalism declined. The whole information organization was in the hands of the propaganda ministry, the Ministry of Popular Culture (MINCULPOP). This ministry decided what was to be printed and published, what photographs were to be included, what line an editorial was to take. Editorial decisions were no longer the responsibility of each editor. Selectivity and a critical faculty were dangerous attributes for an editor who wanted to keep his job. Photography played a large part in the propaganda presentation of events. It was less easy then to photo-graph people without their knowledge, for the photographic equipment was much less sophisticated, but any paper found printing unofficial photographs would be liable to a serious penalty. Journalists were expected to conform.

Mussolini, though no longer an active journalist, contributed articles, books and guide lines on Fascism. Most educated people were expected to read his words. He took an interest in the public relations work that went into promoting his image. He aimed at convincing people that love of country and love of him were the same thing. He hoped that this would hide the fact that he had no hard and fast programme to offer. He did succeed in convincing some of the people some of the time, but, like most illusionists, he did not stand up to careful scrutiny in a crisis.

From his work as a journalist sprang a belief in the power of words. He enjoyed speaking to live audiences and succeeded in establishing a surprising rapport with them. He used slogans, visually and verbally, to get his message over in such a way that it could be easily understood and remembered. He was a vain man whose defects had to be hidden or disguised. He liked to be photographed on horseback, or in such a way as to hide his short stature. Only when he was photographed with the King, Victor Emmanuel, who was even shorter, did he not insist on an angled shot. He shaved his hair when he found he was going bald. He insisted on speaking German to Hitler on his visit to Italy, even though his German was not good enough to be understood, and he refused to allow his age to be mentioned at any of his birthday celebrations. The crowds responded to his magic, chanting at rallies: *"Duce, Duce, Duce, we are yours to the end."* Whatever the occasion demanded, Mussolini would play the part—family man, sportsman, man of the world, man of the people, strong ruler. He always insisted: *"The crowd loves a strong man."* The Secretary of the party put it this way:

God has put his finger on the Duce. He is Italy's greatest son, the rightful heir of Caesar.

This was how Mussolini liked to be regarded. He became obsessed with proving that Italy's past and that of the Mussolini family were intertwined. In his autobiography he wrote:

The Mussolini family was prominent in the city of Bologna in the thirteenth century. . . . Somewhere in the heraldic records there is a Mussolini coat of arms. It has a rather pleasing . . . design . . . six black figures in a yellow field—symbols of valour, courage, force. . . .[4]

His opponents of course did not see him in this patriotic way. Opposition to the regime was not organized. Many emigrated or went into exile, but they were as far from unity then as they had been in the days of his bid for power. A few who remained in Italy risked imprisonment or banishment by joining small bands. They saw through the elaborate image, describing him in this way:

He is a rabbit; a phenomenal rabbit; he roars. Observers who do not know him mistake him for a lion.[3]

Capturing the imagination and loyalty of youth was part of Mussolini's plan. It was not a new idea. The Jesuits had been doing it for centuries, and many countries had Scout and Guide movements, but Fascist youth movements were different. The Fascist way was described by the Secretary of the party:

The regime is and intends to remain a regime of the young. . . . The regime intends to prepare . . . all the youth of Italy, from whom, by successive selections, there must issue the ranks of the governing classes of tomorrow . . . the young of today and tomorrow will be the continuers in spirit and form of the Revolution of October, 1922.[5]

There were Fascist organizations for all ages. For the young there were uniforms, rallies and organized activities to fill in any spare time. Membership was not strictly compulsory but non-members found it harder to get jobs or get on in life, while those who joined found membership a better testimonial than ability. The planners explained:

The young people . . . must be resolutely introduced . . . into the ranks of political, administrative, Trade Union, journalistic, co-operative, academic, sporting life, without jealous stupidity and timorous misconceptions. . . .[5]

Mussolini aimed at training youth for the future and using them in the present to spread the Fascist message among their elders. The youth of Italy were flattered by and attracted to the Fascist party. Being members gave them an identity and cut across class divisions. They felt they were part of a movement that would change society and would value their participation in it. Those in search of excitement and activity found it in the militaristic side of the party. Idealists were drawn to the ideals behind the "Ten Commandments" of Fascism, some of which were:

6. Organize your time in such a way that work will be a joy and your games work.

7. Learn to suffer without complaining, to give without asking, to serve without waiting for a reward.

8. And thank God every day for having made you Fascist and Italian. . . .[5]

Education too was affected by Fascism. Gentile, Minister of Education in 1922, explained:

It is impossible to be a Fascist in politics and not in school. . . .

Textbooks were re-written, expressing the Fascist version of events. History and geography were given a nationalistic bias. In arithmetic, any problem involving area would have the area designated in this way: *"If Mussolini's field measures . . . etc."* Even for infants, traditional story-book characters were replaced by Mussolini. His name and his achievements were included in every aspect of school life. Teachers were expected to be active party members, and, on the surface at least, schools were run on Fascist lines. It was a form of brain washing to turn out good Fascists, who would accept the dictum " *Mussolini is always right*" in any circumstances.

By 1936 Mussolini's dream of an economically self-sufficient Italy had become a nightmare to all but a few who had, like the big industrial groups, made a profit. Mussolini's "battle for births", during which he exhorted Italians to increase the birth rate to achieve a population of 6,000,000 by 1950, merely put extra strain on an already weak economy. Italy was already over populated for its resources and the emigration outlets of old were now closed. His "battle for grain" had some success, a fact that the MINCULPOP emphasized regularly. But, to achieve this, all available land including grazing land and orchards had been put under grain and this reduced the numbers of livestock and the output of other crops, thereby producing a badly out of balance agricultural system.

Despite propaganda concentration on seeming successes, it was becoming harder to explain away the very real and obvious failures,

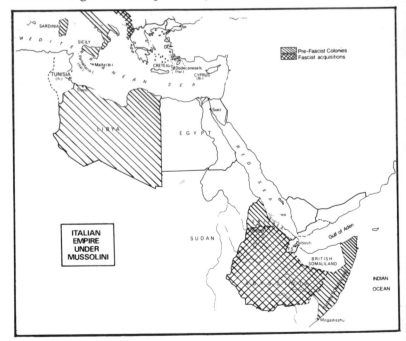

the ones which hit most people's pockets. Failure and corruption were seen in many places and questions were being asked.

Most Italians had backed Mussolini's Abyssinian venture of 1935–36, hoping for new outlets for goods in return for raw materials and increased prestige. It only made the situation worse and certainly did not enhance Italy's prestige. The campaign had been lengthy and costly, supply routes were long, and both as a source of raw materials and a market for goods, the territorial gains did not fulfil expectations. The sanctions which the League of Nations imposed on Italy had little real effect, but they gave Mussolini a chance to call on the people to be patriotic and help their country and he was successful in whipping up support from all quarters, even those in exile. But in the long run it was more of a propaganda exercise than reality. His promises of strong government, stable economy and international prestige had come to nothing. All the pre-Fascist problems were there in greater or lesser degrees and people began to recover their critical faculties.

Mussolini staked his all on a last chance. He tied Italy more tightly to the aggressive and resolute vehicle of Nazi Germany, and embarked on a path to war. Preparations for war helped the economy on a short term basis, particularly that section of the economy involved in heavy industry, whose profits rose. In the long term, however, there was no improvement, but rather the opposite. Mussolini's crowd-appeal was on the wane, and though it improved after his part in the Munich crisis, his hey-day was over. He could not be prevented from taking Italy into war in 1940, against a defeated France, but it was not a popular move. His claim that it was:

War, not for Germany, not with Germany, but beside Germany.
was seen by many as pitiful self-deception. Mussolini said of himself in 1945:

I have gambled right up to the end and I have been beaten. . . .[1]

[1] *Benito Mussolini* by Christopher Hibbert (PENGUIN, 1975); [2] *The Modern World* ed. by Hans Kohn (MACMILLAN N.Y., 1968); [3] *Fascist Italy* by Alan Cassels (THOS. Y. CROWELL, 1969); [4] *My Autobiography* by Benito Mussolini (HURST & BLACKETT, 1937); [5] *Mussolini's Italy* by Herman Finer (FRANK CASS, 1964); [6] *Mussolini and the Rise of Italian Fascism* by R. N. L. Absalom (METHUEN, 1969).

3

Adolf Hitler

The years 1919–23 were crucial ones for the Weimar Republic. It faced tremendous problems and did not have the wholehearted support of many of the German people. It was too moderate for the Left and too tainted with Socialism for the Right. It had too many links with the past for true republicans, and the monarchists hoped it was a temporary measure till Germany was in full control of her own destiny again. Pleasing no one, it could only hope to win support and approval by its actions.

At the time of the Kapp putsch, it hoped for the same support from the army that it had got at the time of the Spartacist rising. It did not get it. By the terms of the treaty, the size of the army had to be cut. Many of the Frei Korps volunteers recruited in 1919 feared that they would be disbanded and end up jobless in a sinking economy. Their officers blamed the Government for this and encouraged by right-wing extremists attempted a putsch. The army looked on, adopting a wait and see attitude, which was neither a vote of confidence for the Government nor a vote of censure for the putsch. The putsch failed, having only half-hearted support and meeting opposition from the trade unions who called a general strike. The Government seemed trapped between the opposing forces of Right and Left and though it gave in to neither, it did nothing to enhance its position.

In the Reichstag only a few parties behaved responsibly and the large number of small parties was a big hindrance to clear-cut programmes being carried through. The change-over to a peace-time economy brought all the usual troubles with restrictions on certain industries and a reduction in the army, making things worse. Unemployment was extensive and inflation, high during the war, grew higher. Wages fell and the cost of living climbed. By 1920 the mark was worth a tenth of its pre-war value against the dollar. People began converting cash into kind in an effort to ward off disaster. In this, some were more successful than others. Anyone with savings in the bank saw them dwindle to nothing. By 1922 the mark had fallen to a hundredth of its old value. Germany had fallen behind on her reparation payments and the French in retaliation had occupied the Ruhr, Germany's big industrial region. It was all but disaster for Weimar. In late 1923, the currency collapsed.

1923	July	October	November
$1 (U.S.) =	160,000M	242,000,000M	4,200,000,000M

On pay days:

> *... people ... dashed to the nearest food store ... when you reached the store a pound of sugar might have been obtainable for two million (marks) but by the time you got to the counter all you could get for two million was half a pound of butter....* [1]

If this was the situation for those in work, it was much worse for the unemployed, old age pensioners, the war disabled, and those on fixed incomes. Savings vanished and the middle classes, who had equated money with power for so long, saw their security and position vanish. What respect they had for Weimar diminished. Feelings were further embittered by the fact that not everyone suffered equally and some even benefited. The big industrialists paid off their debts with the almost worthless currency and rode out the storm. However, the fact that they were able to do this did not mean that they respected the Government any more than before. It was a time of bitterness and despair, and resentment against Versailles and the people who had signed the treaty increased. Membership of extreme parties on the Left and the Right grew. There were Communist uprisings all over Germany and in Munich a right-wing putsch was led by General Ludendorff and a man called Adolf Hitler, supported by the Nazi party.

Adolf Hitler was born in Austria in 1889. He was the son of a minor customs official in the Imperial service. His father, an elderly man, was very much an establishment figure, and he hoped that Adolf would follow in the tradition of service to the State. After an indifferent school career, Hitler went to Vienna hoping to study art. His talent did not match his ambition and the Art School turned him down. He stayed on in the capital, leading an aimless existence and spending much time in the coffee houses which were so much part of Viennese life, and in which much political discussion took place. His parents were both dead and he was in receipt of a pension of 83 kronen a month. Hitler later said:

> *... the allowance which came to me as an orphan was not enough for the bare necessities of life....* [2]

During this time in Vienna most of his later ideas were firmly set in his mind. In particular his anti-Semitism, a very common feeling in Vienna then took a strong hold. It was to become an obsession which grew stronger with the years. Later he said:

Vienna gave me the hardest and most thorough schooling of my whole life....[2]

He never had regular employment, and in later life was to claim that he knew the hardships of the unemployed, having suffered like them. His suffering was voluntary.

In 1913, Hitler left Vienna and turned up later in Munich, the capital of Bavaria. By leaving Austria when he did, he avoided call-up for the Austrian army, but when war broke out in 1914, he joined the Bavarian army. He welcomed the war, saying of it later:

I fell down on my knees and thanked heaven ... for granting me the good fortune of being permitted to live at this time....[2]

He served throughout the war and was decorated for gallantry twice. In the army he found for the first time a purpose in life, comradeship and discipline. The end of the war and the defeat came as a great shock to him and he determined to become a politician. He returned to Munich while still in the army. The city was going through a period of upheaval. A soviet republic had been set up and even in the army there was unrest. Eventually order was restored, but the fear of future Bolshevik trouble made the middle classes and wealthier elements of Munich society particularly sympathetic to any strong group who were avowedly anti-Communist.

Hitler, like many others, condemned the Treaty of Versailles and this condemnation was to be a major part of his political platform. He decided to find some small party which he could mould to his purpose, rather than join a larger, established party which could swamp him. In the course of his army duties he was sent to investigate the German Workers' Party. After the collapse of the Munich soviet, the army were taking no chances and each political group was looked at carefully. Hitler liked what he saw of the party, founded by Anton Drexler. It was small, not very well led nor well organized but Hitler felt that:

There was work to be done and the smaller the party the sooner it could be pulled into shape.[2]

The party members saw in Hitler a personality who could help them. After leaving the army Hitler joined the party and began to mould it into shape. He took over the publicity side and developed his talent for public speaking. He proved a great attraction and in his hands the party membership grew. By 1920, he had renamed it the National Socialist

German Workers' Party—Nazi for short. It was initially only one of many such parties springing up all over Germany, but under Hitler's dynamic leadership the Nazi party grew into something very big. Its early programme was laid down in the "Twenty-five points". It was more positive in its opposition to existing institutions and ideas than it was in putting forward its plans for the future. It was anti-Communist, anti-Weimar, anti-Semitic, anti-Treaty of Versailles, pro-nationalist and vaguely Socialist. Hitler aimed at alienating no one who could be of use to the party, and as he hoped for financial support from the business world, he did not want the Socialist element played up at all. It was there to keep the truly Socialist members of the party satisfied. Hitler wanted power and at this stage was prepared to walk a tightrope to get it.

The Nazi party attracted many different people in its early days. Hitler divided them into those who understood and accepted the aims of the party (followers), and those who were prepared to fight for them (members). One early member explained why he and many like him joined:

We . . . did not join . . . from any rational considerations, or after much contemplation. It was our feelings that led us to Hitler. . . .[3]

The programme wording attracted at least the attention of many, with its recurring: *"We demand . . ."*. It had a positive ring that contrasted with the republican Government's negative impression. A former Nazi, interviewed by Milton Mayer, explained it this way:

National Socialism was a revulsion by my friends against parliamentary politics . . . debate, government—against all the . . . haggling of the parties.[4]

To start with, people joined as a protest against existing conditions, but when Hitler spoke to the crowds he convinced them he was acting for Germany, and this gave the party members and support:

He . . . who once heard him, will never get away from him again. . . .

The Nazi party seemed to offer a way out.

Ex-servicemen joined seeking employment and excitement; the middle classes joined hoping the party could work towards a stable Germany where their old values could have a place; students joined the party seeing it as a hope for the future. After the war many more became students, but the post-war economy meant fewer jobs for those students on graduation. German youth had a long tradition of youth movements, many connected with the churches and political parties, but after the war youth became dissatisfied with these and with how their elders were coping with Germany's troubles. The party attracted to it many eccentric and sadistic men who saw the chance of violence for its own sake, and in the early days of the party there was much street fighting and bloodshed. Hitler, copying Mussolini, developed his Brownshirts, like the Fascist Blackshirts. The Sturmabteilung (Storm Troopers) were the para-military side of the party. They were distinctive in their uniforms with Swastika armbands. They acted as stewards at Nazi meetings and carried war into the enemy camp by heckling and breaking up opposition meetings. They and the S.S. (Schutzstaffel), Hitler's bodyguard, attracted publicity and advertised the party wherever they went. The party thinkers and planners continued to grow in number, but all had to be totally loyal to Hitler.

Financial support came initially from some of the wealthy Munich families, like the Bechsteins and the Hanfstaengls. This money, plus the entrée it gave Hitler into society helped establish him and the party. In November 1923, with Mussolini's march on Rome of 1922 as a blueprint, Hitler decided to attempt a putsch. It failed. Despite the distress of the situation in Germany, the army and the police in Munich held out and the marchers were forced after a short struggle to give in. Hitler was captured and imprisoned. While he was in jail the party was inactive and leaderless, but he re-formed it on his release. This time he did not repeat his mistake. The lesson he learned from the putsch was that he must try to get power by legal means, even if it took time. As he said:

Instead of working to achieve power by armed conspiracy, we shall hold our noses and enter the Reichstag against Catholic and Marxist deputies. If outvoting them takes longer than outshooting them, at least the results will be guaranteed by their own constitution. . . .[5]

The putsch went down in Nazi legend as a noble struggle by a small band of patriots against evil. Those who had been there became heroes. Through time it became almost a sacred victory, and people believed the Nazi version, not the real one.

In the years 1924–29, Hitler continued to build up the party all over Germany, organizing at every level and every walk of life. During this time the party's base grew wider, though Bavaria was to remain the main source of support. It took all Hitler's perseverance to continue developing the party machine. Having said in 1924 that they would enter the Reichstag, it was not till 1928 that the party succeeded in getting twelve deputies into Parliament. However, while they did not have power at that level, the party continued to develop a web of organization all over Germany, building up a pyramid of control from Hitler at the top down to the gauleiters in the districts.

The aim . . . is the greatest possible uniformity . . . in organization and propaganda; the affiliated gauleiters bind themselves in honour . . . to serve the idea of National Socialism under its leader, Adolf Hitler.

Hitler also claimed that what mattered was:

Not the number of Reichstag . . . seats we win, but . . . the extent to which Marxism is destroyed and the degree of enlightenment about its originators, the Jews.

Hitler's attitude to opposition was a mixture of bravado and ridicule. When forbidden to speak in most states in Germany the Nazis produced the poster illustrated below. When the S.A. were forbidden to wear uniform they paraded in underwear.

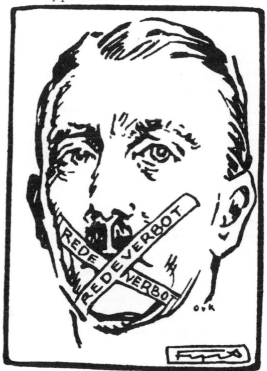

Einer allein von 2000 Millionen Menschen der Erde darf in Deutschland nicht reden!

The caption reads: *"Of all the men in the world, only one is unable to speak."*

Despite the years of waiting, the Nazi party had considerable advantages and Hitler knew this. It was a young party, so could afford to bide its time; nor was it in any way connected with the failures of either the republican regime or the previous regime. It aimed at no one group in society, so could draw on all for support. It was anti-Bolshevik, which commended it to many and it was nationalistic. It was there, just over the horizon, for those who still suffered from the aftermath of 1923, which had shaken what faith they had in the ability of parliamentary government to cope with problems. The bitterness of those times left a large legacy. Hitler was later to claim:

We (the Nazis) are the result of the distress for which others are responsible.

By 1928 there were signs of more economic trouble ahead, and the perennial whipping boy, reparations, came to the fore again. Unemployment was rising and there was widespread economic uncertainty. At the beginning of 1929, a committee met to discuss a final plan for reparations. The word was by now like a red rag to a bull in Germany. The Young Plan set new terms, in return for which Germany would become financially independent again. The plan presupposed continuing economic growth, and the granting of independence was resented by many who felt it was Germany's by right, to be *taken*, not *given* as a favour. The Nazis and the Nationalists, led by a wealthy financier, Alfred Hugenberg, were particularly vocal. The two parties joined forces on this issue and each thought it had made a good bargain. The Nationalists needed the ginger group of Nazi organization; the Nazis needed the respectable front of the Nationalists and they needed Hugenburg's money and influence. With his newspapers and cinemas he could give them a big outlet for their propaganda as well as financial aid.

The next few years of crisis were decisive for Hitler. He and the Nazis were poised to take advantage of events, and the people caught up in the events. The Wall Street Crash of October 1929 affected all Europe, but Germany suffered most. Much of her apparent prosperity was based on short term loans, mainly from America. The crash led to economic ruin and massive unemployment. By 1930 there were three million unemployed and in the crisis, the extremist parties gained support in and out of Parliament. The Communist deputies went up from 57 to 74. The chart on page 35 shows how the Nazi vote rose as unemployment grew. Hitler's insistence on organization and control paid off. The Nazis, unlike the Communists, were ready and more than willing to take advantage of the situation. The end of Weimar was not inevitable at this stage, but the behaviour of the politicians in the crisis helped make it become so. The Nazi party, with its sophisticated propaganda and its flexible programme had the advantage of growing power, but no responsibility. Concern at the

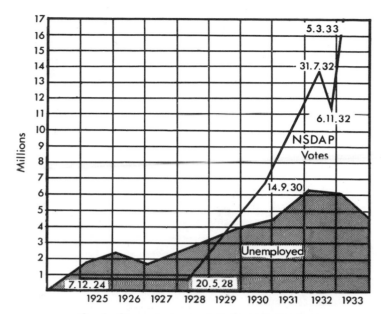

Graph of unemployment and the rise of the Nazis.

possibility of another economic disaster made many people of all classes support them, when at other times they would have thought it out first. In an economic crisis few people think carefully, but tend to look for someone or something to blame, usually the government of the time. If that government is stable, it can usually ride out its unpopularity. The parliamentary regime in Germany at this time was not stable, and it was facing political as well as economic trouble. The politicians did not rise to the occasion. Between 1928 and 1932 there were four elections, as well as numerous cabinet re-shuffles. Chancellors came and went and Article 48 of the constitution was frequently invoked.

While the Nazis did not pick up many votes from the big parties, like the Social Democrats and the Centre party, older voters did defect from the Nationalists and the smaller parties, of which there were many.

The parties representing interest groups, like the German Business party, turned to the Nazis. Middle-class panic gave the Nazis votes. Young people voting for the first time tended to vote Nazi, including a large number of students. Most of the workers who joined the party were unemployed. The overall picture of the party showed a strong lower-middle-class core, a reflection of the fear these people felt for their future under parliamentary government controlled by Weimar politicians. Regionally, the countryside responded better to the Nazi propaganda and electioneering than the industrial areas. It could be argued that this was a case of the more gullible political areas being taken in, but the Government's agrarian policy had failed to give a

Reichstagswahl
Wahlkreis Schleswig-Holstein

1	**Sozialdemokratische Partei Deutschlands** Schroeder, Luise — Eggerstedt — Richter — Diester	1	◯
2	**Deutschnationale Volkspartei** Oberfohren — Gerns — Wülfing von Ditten — Goth	2	◯
3	**Zentrum** Brüning — Häfner — Fuchs, Hedwig — Germeshausen	3	◯
4	**Kommunistische Partei** Thälmann — Augustat, Elise — Heuck — Röhrs	4	◯
5	**Deutsche Volkspartei** Dr. Schifferer — Fischer — Cimbal, Elisabeth — Heims	5	◯
5a	**Christlich-soziale Volksgemeinschaft** Brodersen — Grohinger — Wagner	5a	◯
6	**Deutsche Staatspartei** Paulsen — Dr. Riech-Altenloh, Emilie — Apfeld Ohlrogge	6	◯
7	**Reichspartei des Deutschen Mittelstandes (Wirtschaftspartei)** Köster — Reimers — Musfeldt — Köhler	7	◯
9	**Nationalsozialistische Deutsche Arbeiterpartei (Hitlerbewegung)** Franzen — Meyer-Quade — Thormählen — Stamer	9	◯
10	**Bauern- u. Landvolkpartei Schleswig-Holstein** (Christlich-Nationale Bauern- und Landvolkpartei) Schiele — Köhler — Mangelsen — Bohens	10	◯
11a	**Volksrechtpartei (Reichspartei für Volksrecht und Aufwertung) und Christlich-Soziale Reichspartei** Graf Posadowsky-Wehner—Fleck—Henniger—Kuschert	11a	◯
11b	**Volksrechtpartei** Merks — Mohr — Richter — Roespel	11b	◯
12	**Deutsche Bauernpartei** Leu — Wulff — Harenberg — Wöser	12	◯
16	**Treviranus-Konservative Volkspartei** Treviranus — Lambach — Rieger — von Uhlefeld	16	◯
17	**Christlich-sozialer Volksdienst** Matthiesen — Thiesen — Büntjen — Stolze	17	◯
19a	**Polnische Volkspartei** Ledwolorz — Latoniczak — Zydor — Kwietniewski	19a	◯
19b	**Schleswigscher Verein** Gögaard — Petersen — Iper — Lassen	19b	◯
19c	**Friesland** Oldsen — Henningsen — Petersen — Lorenzen	19c	◯
23	**Unabhängige Sozialdemokratische Partei Deutschlands** Liebknecht — Wiegmann, Elsa — Helder — Schröder	23	◯
24	**Haus- und Grundbesitzer** Wehner — Kohlmorgen — Krabad — Schramm	24	◯
28	**Menschheitspartei und Neue Volksgemeinschaft** Heydorn — Reimpell — Thiel — Duus	28	◯

A ballot paper for Schleswig-Holstein in 1930.

boost to agriculture, and bankruptcy for even one in a small isolated community could mean disaster for all. In the towns most of the workers were Socialist or Communist, and were also more politically sophisticated. The trade unions were not in favour of National Socialism. The industrialists were mainly concerned to support the group most likely to give Germany stability. Weimar's handling of events worried them and they kept a careful eye on Nazi successes.

Though the crisis in government was to Hitler's advantage, he had the problem of restraining the extremists of his party who wanted to seize power by a *coup*, rather than follow his "legal" approach. Though Hitler had great support, it was not overwhelming and he feared a repetition of the 1923 putsch. It was safer to play a waiting game and force his opponents into errors, than to rush at this stage into an uncertain position. In any case, he did not want to be black-mailed, if the *coup* succeeded, by those carrying it out. It was not easy as time dragged on to restrain the S.A. followers, unemployed, spoiling for a fight and under the control of Ernst Roehm, who wanted revolution, but Hitler succeeded. The election campaigns were fought hard and violently by the Nazis and the German people were bombarded with posters.

Self-interest and conceit by those in power stopped any con-structive policy coming from the Reichstag. In January 1933, President Hindenburg was reluctantly compelled by the cabinet to ask Hitler to try to form a government. He was, as Alan Bullock put it *"jobbed into office by a backstairs intrigue"*, by politicians like Franz von Papen. *"We have hired Hitler"* was Papen's cynical comment. Such cynicism goes a long way to explain how the Weimar Republic failed.

Many people saw hope for Germany with Hitler taking over as Chancellor. He had presented a vigorous, powerful image, and people, tired of the drabness and indecision of Weimar politicians, felt he should be given a chance. One German commented:

. . . Hitler is Chancellor of the Reich! And what a cabinet . . . National Socialist drive, German national reason, the non-political Stahlhelm, not to forget Papen. . . . What a great thing Hindenburg has achieved. . . .[6]

Once Hitler became leader of Germany he was to claim that he got there by the overwhelming will of the German people, but facts disprove this. By the second of the elections in 1932 the Nazi vote had dropped, as had their numbers in the Reichstag. As we have seen, intrigue won him office and the Enabling Bill gave him power. Once it was passed by the Reichstag, Weimar was finished. Hitler, in his role of attempting to govern democratically, called an election in

These two posters show opposite views of Hitler and the Nazis. (1) shows the Nazi as Superman; (2) shows Hitler as a butcher leading cattle to the slaughter.

March 1933. Despite having all the power of the State behind them, the Nazis did not get an overall majority. Clearly Hitler had been wise to use his "legal" path to power, rather than a putsch, which would have shown his intentions and might well have united the opposition firmly against him. As it was, he destroyed them by a mixture of intimidation and opportunism. The Reichstag fire of 1933 gave Hitler the chance to destroy Communist opposition and appear to be acting in the interests of the country. Claiming the fire was part of a Communist plot, he had all leading Communists, in and out of Parliament, arrested. With the Communists out of Parliament and Nazi S.A. and S.S. troops outside the Opera House in Berlin, where the Reichstag was meeting, the scene was set for a Nazi victory. In 1928 Goebbels had said:

We (the Nazis) will move into the Reichstag to supply ourselves at the arsenal of democracy with its own weapons . . . we will become deputies of the Reichstag to paralyse the Weimar way of thinking . . . we do not come as friends. We come as enemies.

The Enabling Bill brought the paralysis. By intimidation it was forced through Parliament by 441 votes to 94. Only the Social Democrats had the courage to vote against it. Hitler now had the power he needed, and he had got it by due parliamentary process, on the surface at least. The Act stated:

The Reich cabinet is authorized to enact laws . . . laws enacted by the

Reich cabinet shall be prepared by the Chancellor . . . they will come into effect the following day.

Germany became a one party State and, after Hindenburg's death in 1934, it became a dictatorship, with Adolf Hitler as *Fuehrer*. Having come to power, Hitler wanted to rid himself of troublesome elements in the party, namely Roehm and the S.A. who saw themselves as the nucleus of the new army. The army had stood aside in 1933, during the crisis; self-preservation was again their motive, but in return they wanted security of tenure. The industrialists too wanted to dispose of the S.A. and the Socialist threat. All these interested parties were satisfied after 30 June 1934, when the *"Night of the Long Knives"* removed Roehm and other S.A. leaders, as well as many others whose presence annoyed Hitler and his close associates. Justification was produced in the shape of yet another plot against the State.

The trade unions were disposed of in 1933. Leading union officials likely to give trouble were imprisoned. Workers were forbidden to strike and collective bargaining was banned. This pleased the industrialists, who increased their support of Hitler. The workers were organized by the German Labour Front, which directed their hours of work, place of work and pay. The "Kraft durch Freude" (Strength through Joy) movement organized their leisure time, and their lack of freedom was sweetened by providing welfare services and subsidised holidays abroad. Though wages were pegged, prices were too, and this, plus benefits and holidays, was expected to keep the workers quiet.

The economic problem was tackled by a Four Year Plan. With prices and wages pegged, inflation declined and this kept the middle classes happy. The Plan allowed for State financial aid for a road building programme, house building, and land drainage which gave more opportunities for agriculture. The autobahn plan gave Germany a fine road system. Cheap houses allowed the State to encourage young people to marry early and have large families. There were even marriage grants and prizes for mothers of large families. Indirectly this took young women off the labour market and left jobs open for men. All the schemes meant a big reduction in unemployment, which satisfied the workless supporters of the party. Young people were conscripted to work on the land. This not only gave them employment; it also meant they could be fed with propaganda to spread among others.

Hitler had always attacked the Treaty of Versailles. Now, in power, he had the chance to act. In defiance of the terms, a massive re-armament programme was started. This created work for thousands and helped to restore German self-confidence. By 1938, there were more jobs than men to fill them. Coupled with the re-introduction of conscription it delighted the High Command. With one stroke Hitler seemed to satisfy many people and cure Germany's ills. Caught up in the enthusiasm of the time many did not look too closely at what all this direction of labour implied.

Propaganda played a big part in the seeming recovery of Germany. It had always been one of Hitler's major weapons, and backed up by strict censorship it was carried to new heights. Hitler had little respect for the masses, yet he preferred addressing them to face to face discussions. He wrote in 1924:

The receptive ability of the masses is very limited, their understanding is small; on the other hand they have a great power of forgetting . . . all effective propaganda must be confined to a very few points. . . .[2]

He was also an advocate of telling a big lie rather than a little one, believing that if it were big enough no one would think it could be other than true. He realized that mass audiences were more likely to be swayed by emotion than reason. In his address to the Party Congress in 1936 he said:

What would they have said (his opponents of 1933) if I had prophesied that before the end of four years, 99% of this nation, which was at that time so torn asunder, would exercise their right to vote and that 99% of those would record their vote in favour of the Nazi policy of reconstruction, honour and freedom of the nation. . . .

People accepted this and believed it, despite the hollowness of the claim. Elections were not free. Voting was compulsory and there was only one party for which to vote. Indoctrination and propaganda conditioned people to be uncritical. The Nazis had practised it during their years of waiting. They had published newspapers and journals, held rallies and exploited every available chance with posters and speeches to reach as wide and varied an audience as possible. Once they were in power, they had unlimited resources at their disposal.

The Swastika was both a badge and an advertisement, used on flags, armbands and back drops for meetings. The Ministry of Propaganda was in the hands of Joseph Goebbels, a most able propagandist. By the use of propaganda and censorship, he was able, at Hitler's direction, to manipulate the facts to suit the party. Editors of the big daily papers in Berlin attended briefing sessions about editorial policy. Hitler had his official photographer, Hoffmann, who kept a photographic record of the Fuehrer's activities. Hitler decided what should or should not be published. He aimed at being a father figure and, at the same time, a man of destiny, aloof from his people yet understanding their needs. His appearances were greeted enthusiastically wherever he went. Cheer-leaders ensured that.

Censorship led inevitably to the banning of books and art which were not characteristically Nazi. Book-burning was a common part of life in the early years of Nazi power. Thus, where Weimar Germany had had a thriving and varied cultural life, Nazi Germany did not.

The one part of the propaganda programme which more than any other gave entertainment and spectacle was the annual rally held at Nuremberg. Nuremberg was chosen because of its connection with Germany's past and with Wagnerian legend. It was also a junction town for road and rail and so was easy to reach. All the leaders came to take turns at addressing the crowds, leading up to the last night and Hitler's appearance. Planning and precision made the marching and parades a spectacle of efficiency, and community singing of Nazi songs to traditional German tunes made the experience a moving one. William Shirer, an American correspondent at the time, described it in *Berlin Diary*:

After seven days of almost ceaseless goose-stepping, speechmaking and pageantry the party rally came to an end. . . . They looked upon him (Hitler) as if he were a Messiah, their faces transformed into something positively inhuman. . . . You have to go through one of these to understand Hitler's hold over the people and the sheer disciplined strength the Germans possess. . . .[7]

Propaganda was used to attract people. Organization was used to control them as Nazi party members. There were Nazi groups for all ages and all interests and occupations. The groundwork was done in the years before power and once in power they grew in strength. Party members progressed; non-members were made to feel excluded and they did not find life or work easy. Hitler aimed at replacing all other loyalties to family, churches and employers by total loyalty to the Nazis.

To be a National Socialist means nothing but: Fight, Faith, Work, Sacrifice.[3]

In particular, German youth was subjected to a rigorous campaign of indoctrination. A law of 1936 stated:

The entire German youth within the boundaries of the Reich is organized in the Hitler Youth. It is not only in the home and school, but in the Hitler Youth as well that all of Germany's youth is to be educated, physically, mentally, and morally, in the spirit of National Socialism. . . .[3]

Conditioned as Germans always had been to the idea of youth movements, most saw the attractions but not the intention behind the Nazi scheme. Young people were encouraged to mix with each other, to join in activities which were healthy and enjoyable, hiking, swimming, camping, athletics, community service. Marching and uniforms appealed to all and gave excitement and entertainment. The movement gave them a sense of belonging. It gave the Nazi party a great opportunity for publicizing the party message, many youthful disciples to spread the message, as well as a hard core of loyal Nazis for the future struggles.

Education played a large part in this. Dr Rust, the Education Minister explained:

The whole function of education is to create Nazis.

The whole educational system and its books were re-structured on Nazi lines. There was no room for discussion. The motto for youth was:

"Fuehrer, command, we follow."

Another general aspect of education which the Nazis opposed was religion. Germany had a long history of religious intolerance, with Protestantism dominant in the north and Catholicism in the south. Both Churches supported Hitler initially as the legal Head of State. Hitler used the Churches and their rituals to suit himself, but avoided direct confrontation with them. Propaganda photographs of priests or pastors taking part in any Nazi parade or ceremony were distributed widely. However, Martin Bormann, Hitler's aide, said publicly:

National Socialism and Christian concepts are irreconcilable. . . .

Hitler saw Christianity as a rival and intended to replace the Churches with a National Church.

Never again must influence over leadership of the people be yielded to the Churches

was his vow.

Against members of the Jewish faith or race, he was fanatical in his hatred. The Jews were his perpetual scapegoat, taking the blame for all Germany's ills. They were systematically shut out of German life, forbidden to be German.

A law of 1935 read:

Jews are not permitted to display the German flag or the national colours. . . . They are . . . permitted to show the Jewish colours. The exercise of this right is protected by the state. . . .[3]

What began as cruelty and persecution ended in attempted annihilation in concentration camps.

These photographs show two aspects of a rally at Nuremberg. In (1) the ranks of uniformed Storm Troopers stand at attention before the speakers' rostrum; in (2) the crowds greet Hitler enthusiastically.

The notice in this photograph, which reads *"Jews not wanted here"*, sums up the Nazi and German attitude.

Concentration camps took care of opposition to Hitler; the first ones were established in 1933. People did not ask too closely about them or those sent to them. The Gestapo and the S.S. had woven a web of informers all over Germany. This made criticism as well as opposition difficult. Reprisals were carried out not only on the victims but on their families too. Even suspicion of opposition was enough. Hitler maintained that:

We have to put a stop to the idea that it is part of everybody's civil right to say whatever he pleases.

There was always underground opposition to Hitler, but it was not till the war that it became organized. When it failed, the punishment meted out was an awful warning to others.

Fed with propaganda, their self-respect restored and prosperity re-established, the German people seemed to have recovered from their Weimar doldrums. Hitler's Four Year Plan seemed successful. Successes abroad added to his popularity and made it harder for his critics to argue against him. His speeches made the Germans feel superior, with his talk of the Master Aryan Race, the position of Germany in the future when "lebensraum" in the East of Europe would give them living space and slave races to do the work.

Until 1942 Hitler seemed to have succeeded and by then the German people were too committed to do anything other than continue to support the Nazis. Their only hope, so they were told, was to wage total war. Whatever happened, there was no way out. Yet Hitler, in his last testament written before his suicide in 1945, wrote: *I die with a happy heart, conscious of the immeasurable deeds and achievements of our soldiers . . . of our Youth, who bear my name. . . .*[6]

---

[1]*Der Fuehrer* by Konrad Heiden (HENRY PORDES, 1967); [2]*Mein Kampf* by Adolf Hitler, tr. R. Manheim (HUTCHINSON, 1972); [3]*The Nazi Years* by Joachim Remak (PRENTICE-HALL, 1969); [4]*They Thought They Were Free: The Germans 1933-45* by Milton Mayer (UNIVERSITY OF CHICAGO PRESS, 1966); [5]*I Knew Hitler* by Kurt Ludecke (JARROLD); [6]*Documents on Nazism 1919-45* ed. by Noakes & Pridham (CAPE, 1974); [7]*Berlin Diary* by William Shirer (SPHERE, 1970).

Contrasts and Comparisons

At first sight, an alliance between Hitler and Mussolini seemed inevitable. They were the only right-wing dictators in Europe at the time. They were, by 1936, both out of favour with other European powers. Both were leaders of totalitarian regimes, both had territorial ambitions, with Austria the only area in which both had an interest, and as such, seemed to have much in common. Hitler had hero worshipped Mussolini in the days when the latter was established and the former a struggling politician.

This seeming similarity of outlook did not apply to the peoples they led, nor, on close scrutiny, to the regimes. Italy and Germany were no more alike in the inter-war years than they had been at the time of unification. Their peoples neither trusted nor liked each other. Most Germans still agreed with Bismarck's comment that political relationship with the Italians was impossible as they were equally untrustworthy as friends or foes. And many Italians endorsed Mussolini's early comment;

> *Thirty centuries of history allow us to regard with supreme indulgence certain doctrines taught beyond the Alps, by the descendants of people who were wholly illiterate in the days when Caesar . . . flourished in Rome. . . .*[1]

The Rome-Berlin Axis was based more on self-interest than identity of interest. It developed into a personal alliance, compounded of a natural curiosity and an element of rivalry.

Both men came from a lower-middle-class background, an unlikely source, at the time of their birth, for future rulers. Mussolini grew up in an atmosphere of radical politics and was an avowed Socialist from his early youth. This commitment to the Left was later to make him suspect to the extremists of his own Fascist party. It did affect his attitude to the Socialists once he came to power and had recovered from the shock of being expelled from the party in 1914. Near the end of his life he admitted:

The bourgeois, with their materialistic mentality are the ruin of Italy.
I am an old Socialist at heart![1]

Hitler, on the other hand, was brought up in a reactionary atmosphere with little political interest. During his years in Vienna, he took part in many political discussions at coffee house level, but he joined no party. He believed firmly in a Pan-German nationalism, and, Austrian by birth, was not a true native of the country he ruled. Where Mussolini was obsessed by his ancestors, Hitler was reticent. In *his* role as a man of destiny, where he came from did not matter. To Mussolini, in *his* role of the Italian patriot, it did.

Mussolini was well-travelled. He spoke French and English, not fluently enough for speechmaking, but enough for conversation. He had read widely and could be a good conversationalist. Hitler's travels were much more limited. He was unknown outside Germany until the 1920s and spoke only German, with a marked Austrian accent. This was a source of pride rather than shame to him. His knowledge of literature was limited and he preferred monologues to the give and take of conversation.

He came to politics at a later age than Mussolini and did not have any experience of parliamentary politics. As an Austrian, he was not eligible to stand for the Reichstag, but preferred to be outwith the confines of Parliament. He was more consistent in his attitudes than Mussolini. He had welcomed the war in 1914 and once he committed himself politically, did not waver. He said in November, 1933:

I did not become Chancellor in order to act otherwise than I have preached for fourteen long years.[2]

Mussolini had longer political experience to draw on and had served as a deputy in Parliament. He seemed the more likely of the two to succeed and to be the dominant one of any partnership they might have.

Post-war conditions were similar in both countries, despite one being the victor and the other the loser. However, Germany had experienced revolution and Italy had not. As a result, it took longer for Hitler to establish himself. Having regained control, the German Government, the Civil Service and the army had good reasons for keeping a firm hand on affairs and any suspected trouble-makers were investigated and dealt with. It was on an errand of this kind that Hitler had found the party he made into the Nazi one. In Italy pre-war corruption continued, with wavering incompetence giving in to what seemed to be the strong positive force of Fascism. Hitler, who had watched Mussolini's progress carefully, modelled his *coup* of 1923 in

Munich on the Fascist march on Rome of the previous year. He failed to realize that Mussolini's coming to power owed as much to the weakness of the King and Government as to Mussolini's strength. He found out too that in Germany, reactions were not the same as in Italy and that economic distress and an unpopular government were not sufficient reasons for people to join him and win, if the police and the army stood firm. Mussolini's success had been against an inactive army and an incompetent, corrupt police force.

Though he had learned his lesson in 1923, Hitler, when he re-formed the Nazi party, continued to model it on Mussolini's Fascists. His S.A. wore brown shirts; the Fascists wore black shirts. The Roman salute was adopted in 1926 and even in his choice of a symbol for the party he copied Mussolini and took it from antiquity, rather than devising one of his own. Just as the Fascists used violence in the streets to intimidate their opponents and give a warning to onlookers, the Nazi bands did so too. Like the Fascists they were tough thugs, but there was a greater element of sadism in Nazi street fights. Where the Fascists used rubber truncheons and castor oil, the Nazis used metal truncheons and bullets. Hitler described one attack:

... my Storm Troopers ... attacked like wolves and they flung themselves on their enemies ... after only five minutes I saw hardly one of them not covered in blood ... wild shooting began. ... Your heart rejoiced at such a revival of old war experiences. ...[2]

In both countries the post-war era was one of savagery on the part of the strong-arm bands of all political parties. The Fascists in Italy and the Nazis in Germany were simply better at it and while by comparison the Nazis were the more ruthless, the terror both groups created was the same.

Keeping the hotheads of the party under control was a problem both men had to face. Both wanted power to come to them, but they backed their judgment as to timing. Both succeeded in keeping the initiative. Once in power, they differed in the way in which they reacted to pressure from extremists. Mussolini allowed himself to be forced to assume dictatorial powers by the extremists after the Matteotti affair. This stripped him of his cloak of legality and ensured the end of compromise. Mussolini's inclination was the same as the extremists, but his timing was not.

Hitler moved more swiftly towards dictatorship and squashed any opposition in the party which might pressure him into more socialism than he wanted. The "*Night of the Long Knives*" was his answer to pressure. He had not come to power legally to give in to men like

Roehm. At the same time he was able to get rid of the S.A. who were an embarrassment in power, just as they had been very useful on the way to power. Transition from opposition to power was smooth in Germany. Long preparation and methodical planning played some part, but the speed with which Hitler disposed of opposition helped too. Six months was all he took to control German life, except the army, and that came too, in August 1934. Hitler did not compromise, nor did he try to work within the system. He proceeded to introduce totalitarianism bit by bit. It was an insidious movement with social and economic re-construction on one hand balancing terror on the other. Those who did not fall foul of the Nazis supposedly enjoyed improved living standards, good employment prospects and the hope of prosperity and stability. Few questioned the basis for this prosperity. It was there, and after so long without it, the German people were happy to accept. Those who did not fit in to the Nazi scheme received harsh treatment. The S.S. and the Gestapo quickly established a police state. Hitler issued warnings in his speeches:

Let it be known for all time . . . that if anyone raises his hand to strike the State, then certain death is his lot.[2]

Mussolini and the Fascists were less organized and less efficient in their attitude to opposition. There was more tolerance on the whole and the violence was sporadic rather than consistent. It was nevertheless part of the Fascist State. Exile or imprisonment in one of the penal colonies was the fate for most who opposed Mussolini; death was the fate for a few. Mussolini did not achieve the smooth change-over from opposition to government. At first he worked within the existing framework and even when he became dictator, the monarchy and the Upper House remained, as figure-heads admittedly, but there nonetheless. Mussolini was less successful too in his economic policy. He did not succeed, despite all his advantages, in solving Italy's economic troubles. The schemes and promises were grandiose, yet might have been fulfilled given application and efficiency. In practice, the age old problem of inefficiency and corruption put paid to most of the plans. Though not acquisitive himself, most of his officials were, and where there was not bribery there was inefficiency and weak control. Once he had launched a scheme and the novelty had worn off, Mussolini lost interest. Provided his speeches told of successful schemes, he could believe they were as he described them. It was a dangerous economic maxim for Italy: "*Mussolini is always right.*" He was never able to move away from the origins of the Fascists—war, unrest, violence. Without the challenge these gave, he was unable to find another formula. As the ruler of Italy, he did not get his priorities right; Hitler did. When Hitler embarked on international activities, he did so from the security of a sound economy. While hoping for success, he knew failure would not be too costly to Germany and success would be an added bonus for his popularity and his country's self-respect. Until 1939, he counted the cost accurately.

Mussolini, encouraged by Hitler for his own reasons, embarked on imperial expansion in Ethiopia. He found it very costly. It ruined the economy, which was already shaky. It was a mitigated success, which did little for his popularity or Italian self-confidence and it lost Italy power and respect in Europe. It also upset the balance of power in Europe and put him firmly in Hitler's hands.

Mussolini had always upheld the need for Austria as a buffer state against German expansion in Italy's direction. In 1925 and 1930 he had stated this firmly. The two countries shared a common frontier and a common religion, Catholicism. By 1936, he could no longer uphold these statements. He had a weakened economy, was under threat of sanctions by the League of Nations and was out of favour with Britain and France. Hitler rescued his pride by offering help to beat sanctions and an alliance to restore his self-respect. The price was non-intervention when Hitler decided to annexe Austria. Hitler also gained the satisfaction of scrapping yet more of the Treaty of Versailles and "cocking a snook" at the League of Nations. The Rome-Berlin partnership was sealed. To make sure that Italy remained the junior partner, Hitler encouraged Mussolini to support Franco's forces in the Spanish Civil War. Mussolini responded by sending large numbers of troops which Italy could ill afford to train or equip, thus keeping the economy weak. Hitler, by contrast, restricted his aid to the "Condor Squadron" and kept well within his means.

What had begun as a friendship of Mussolini, the Father of Italian Fascism, and recognized dictator, with Hitler, newly appointed Chancellor of Germany, and a newcomer to power, became in 1936 an alliance in which Hitler was the dominant figure and Mussolini the poor relation. Though the two continued to act independently of each other as leaders, at a personal level they professed friendship. Hitler said after the annexation of Austria:

> . . . tell Mussolini that I will never forget him for this. . . . I shall stick to him . . . even if the whole world were against him. . . .[3]

When that eventually happened, Hitler kept his promise, and Mussolini said:

> I knew that my friend Adolf Hitler would not desert me.

As a person, Hitler was friendly to Mussolini. As a leader, he put his interests first and was to regret "the brutal friendship".

Once Hitler had come to power, Mussolini gave in to a natural curiosity to meet the man who had admired him and his party for so long. He agreed to Hitler's proposal for a meeting.

Their first encounter did not seem hopeful. Mussolini condescended to Hitler and outshone him in elaborate uniforms while Hitler wore civilian dress. To Mussolini, Hitler seemed like a "garrulous monk" who was harmless and posed little danger as a personality to his own brilliance. He misjudged him. When the return visit was made by Mussolini to Germany, he was overwhelmed by the power and efficiency of the whole country. It was superior, and he knew it, to anything Italy could offer. No longer would he state:

The Germans should allow themselves to be guided by me if they wish to avoid unpardonable blunders. . . .[1]

In their love of display, their leadership cult and their use of propaganda as well as violence, they were alike. They were concerned to present the right image to the public. Both made sure that unflattering publicity of any kind was stopped. Heinrich Hoffmann, Hitler's photographer, kept a better visual record of the Fuehrer, but Mussolini made sure that there were pictures to go with all the moods and abilities he wanted the public to know about. Rallies and large gatherings of any sort were the occasions which both men used to display their talents as speakers. They both played on the emotions of the audience, both practising gestures and speeches beforehand to give the impression of spontaneity. Little was left to chance. The difference in the two performances was in the degree of planning efficiency. As usual, the Germans were the better. Though they both used crowds to put over their propaganda, their attitude to them did vary, Hitler's being the more cynical of the two. Mussolini claimed that:

The crowd loves strong men . . . everything turns upon one's ability to control it like an artist. . . .[1]

whereas Hitler, as we saw in Chapter 3, felt that the receptive power was small and their understanding feeble.

Just as Mussolini's remark showed more concern for himself as a performer, he had greater need of the ubiquitous slogan *"Mussolini is always right."* Hitler did not indulge in such a slogan. As Schacht, the Reichsbank President, put it:

The thing that impressed me most about this man was his absolute conviction of the rightness of his outlook. . . .

Of the two, Hitler commanded deeper loyalty from his followers and this let him carry Germany with him to the end. Only in the days before defeat in 1945 did some defect, whereas Mussolini was betrayed by some of his closest associates as early as 1943. The Nazi party was much more a party of "personalities" than the Fascist one. Hitler had round him men like Goering, Goebbels, Hess and Himmler, yet he remained at all times undisputed leader. Germany was more conditioned to the "leader" cult, and there was a tradition of local government loyalty and efficiency, totally lacking in Italy. Bribery and intimidation had always played a part in Italian local government and this tradition continued under the Fascist "ras". Though there was never the total uniformity in Germany that propaganda implied, there was not the corruption and independent action there was in Italy. The gauleiters were appointed after careful training in loyalty to the Fuehrer.

Mussolini's Fascism had none of the racial tones of Nazism. Though it was nationalistic, it did not subscribe to the "Master Race" theory and it was more tolerant of other races. There was little anti-Semitism in Italy. The many Jews who had settled there had become absorbed and were looked on as Italians. Their different diet and way of life was acknowledged, but not resented. Even when, in response to Hitler, Mussolini did introduce some anti-Semitic laws, they were neither promulgated nor enforced with enthusiasm.

The attitude of the two men to religion was different. Where Mussolini envisaged a Church within the State, Hitler planned a National Church to take the place of other churches. Mussolini said of the situation in Italy:

> *Fascism gives impulse and vigour to the religion of the country . . . but will never be able . . . to renounce the sovereign rights . . . and functions of the State.*[4]

His position was a different one in that Italy was Catholic and the Papacy was situated within Italy's borders. As always, there was strong outside interest in the position of the Catholic faith in Italy, and this was bound to have an effect. Hitler did not have this limiting influence, nor was Germany a wholly Catholic country. This view was made clear when he stated:

> *A politician . . . must estimate the value of a religion, not so much in connection with its faults . . . but in relation to the advantages of a substitute which may be manifestly better.*[5]

Education was an important part of Hitler's and Mussolini's plans. Hitler had greater control over it, because the Churches had no part in education. In Italy, under the Lateran Agreement, Mussolini had agreed to religious education in schools and the retention of church schools. Nevertheless, both men felt indoctrination through education was a safeguard for the future. Censorship put another limitation on education, as it also limited cultural life. There was much more tolerance on Mussolini's part, though many books were banned. However, critics of his regime did not automatically face imprisonment or exile. As a writer of some ability he once said:

> *I wouldn't complain if there was even one good Fascist book. But what have we had? Ill-written clap-trap. I'd rather have well-written abuse than that.*[1]

The Italians were too tolerant and casual about the non-conformists to suffer the excesses of Hitler's Germany, but censorship in culture did have a serious effect.

Propaganda, a forceful weapon, was successful for both men because it was backed by censorship, which took away the chance of comparison with unbiased or differently biased views. It was also part of the entertainment value of the two parties. Italy and Germany's past glories were re-told to build up people's self-confidence and the drab reality of the immediate past contrasted with the image of the promised land conjured up by Hitler and Mussolini, who promised Italians a return to the days of Rome as *the* power centred in the Mediterranean.

The visual side of entertainment was emphasized on every possible occasion, with audience participation as well as spectator entertainment. Meetings and parades gave people excitement, whether they were actively involved or merely onlookers. Well-trained formations of Storm Troopers or Fascist squads, accompanied by bands playing good rousing tunes were an excellent advertisement. At rallies, there was community singing of all the propaganda songs, *tableau vivants* were organized and part of the ritual which gave a quasi-religious aspect to every gathering was the audience responses, usually led by carefully placed "cheer-leaders". Fascist rallies resounded to chants of *"Duce, Duce, Duce, we are yours to the end"*, while at Nazi rallies the cry was *"Sieg Heil, Ein Volk, Ein Reich, Ein Fuehrer"*. They were deliberately arranged emotional occasions during which slogans and symbols continually reminded the people of the regime.

Both men were able to take advantage of the widening chances for youth to take an active part in political life. Post-war youth became a social and political force. This was possible because of greater educational facilities, which meant more students. Cheaper mobility allowed travel and increased opportunities for meeting and mixing. Changes in working conditions allowed more leisure time and universal franchise gave the young a say in politics. Both Hitler and Mussolini were able to take advantage of this by attracting youth to parties which had no previous connection with government and were looked on with suspicion by the older generation. This was an attraction in itself and when many of the young found themselves with no jobs, they turned to the most outspoken critics of existing power. Having attracted them in the first place Hitler and Mussolini set about keeping them and indoctrinating them for the future. Hitler was the more successful of the two. In Italy, however, the Fascist youth movement had to contend with the Church either as a rival or a stumbling block.

Just as a definition of Fascism or Nazism is all but impossible and an explanation of them as phenomena difficult, the two men who inspired them are and have been very difficult to analyse. One of Mussolini's associates described him in this way:

By turns shrewd and innocent, brutal and gentle, vindictive and forgiving, great and petty, he is the most complicated and contradictory man I have ever known. He cannot be explained.[1]

Joseph Goebbels, a close friend of Hitler, described him this way:

He is like a child, kind, good, merciful; like a cat, cunning, clever, agile; like a lion, roaring, great and gigantic. . . .

John Wheeler-Bennett, an eminent historian of the Western Dictators wrote:

If one accepts the principle that everything is comparative, within these limits Mussolini was a "nicer" man than Hitler. The Duce had not the black heart of the Fuehrer, or, if he had, it was a lighter shade of black. Hitler was cold, humourless, fanatical and dedicated. He spoke no language but his own. Though he had written a book (Mein Kampf) of historical importance, I doubt if he ever read for pleasure. . . . Mussolini, on the other hand, had an essentially warm personality. He was a human being with all the failings and a few of the virtues. . . . He was a semi-sophisticated blackguard. . . .[6]

---

[1]*Benito Mussolini* by Christopher Hibbert (PENGUIN, 1975); [2]*Hitler* by Joachim C. Fest, tr. R. & C. Winston (WEIDENFELD & NICOLSON, 1974); [3]*Documents on Nazism 1919–45* ed. by Noakes & Pridham (CAPE, 1974); [4]*My Autobiography* by Benito Mussolini (HURST & BLACKETT, 1937); [5]*Mein Kampf* by Adolf Hitler, tr. R. Manheim (HUTCHINSON, 1972); [6]*Knaves, Fools and Heroes* by Sir John Wheeler-Bennett (MACMILLAN, 1974).

Assignments

1. Imagine that you are a teacher of history, married, with two children. You and your family live in Heidelberg, and you have a number of other relatives in the town. You are not a Nazi, but your headmaster is. You are asked to teach Nazi history. You cannot afford to retire, or to leave the country. What do you do?

Arrange yourselves in family groups of four and discuss this problem. Having done so, appoint a spokesman to give the family decision and the reasons for it.

2. The following were oaths of loyalty sworn by the German armed forces at different times. The FIRST one was the oath taken during the time of the Weimar Republic; the SECOND one was the oath taken after Adolf Hitler became Fuehrer. There are significant differences in the two oaths. Make a list of those you can identify. Bearing those in mind, why do you think Hitler made the changes?

I swear loyalty to the Constitution. I vow that I will protect the German nation and its lawful establishments as a brave soldier at any time and will be obedient to the President and my superiors.

I swear by God this sacred oath: I will render unconditional obedience to Adolf Hitler, Fuehrer of the German nation and people, Supreme Commander of the Armed Forces, and will be ready as a brave soldier to risk my life at any time for this oath.

. . . The National Socialist movement, assembled, at this hour, as a fighting squad around its leader, today calls on the entire German people to join its ranks, and to pave a path that will bring Adolf Hitler to the head of the nation, and thus

Lead Germany to Freedom.

Hitler Is the password of all who believe in Germany's resurrection.

Hitler Is the last hope of those who were deprived of everything: of farm and home, of savings, employment, survival; and who have but one possession left: their faith in a just Germany which will once again grant to its citizens honor, freedom, and bread.

Hitler Is the word of deliverance for millions, for they are in despair, and see only in this name a path to new life and creativity.

Hitler Was bequeathed the legacy of the two million dead comrades of the World War, who died not for the present system of the gradual destruction of our nation, but for Germany's future.

Hitler Is the man of the people hated by the enemy because he understands the people and fights for the people.

Hitler Is the furious will of Germany's youth, which, in the midst of a tired generation, is fighting for new forms, and neither can nor will abandon its faith in a better German future. Hence Hitler is the password and the flaming signal of all who wish for a German future.

All of them, on March 13, will call out to the men of the old system who promised them freedom and dignity, and delivered stones and words instead: We have known enough of you. Now you are to know us!

Unsere letzte Hoffnung: HITLER

3. The poster opposite was used by the Nazi Party in the election of March 1932.

a. Bearing in mind the disunity of the Weimar Republic, what impression is conveyed by the opening passage?

b. The phrase "Hitler is our *password*" is used at two points. What do you think was the reason for using this particular term?

c. Why would it be an advantage for Hitler to be linked with the views of "... the two million dead comrades of the World War"?

d. What does Hitler hope to gain by identifying himself as the man "hated by the enemy"?

e. How many separate groups is the poster appealing to?

f. There are many phrases in the poster which have a religious significance. At least eight are to be found. List as many as you can see.

THEY SALUTE WITH BOTH HANDS NOW

4. This cartoon was published in the London *Evening Standard* in July 1934, after the "*Night of the Long Knives*".

What do you think is the significance of Hitler's armband?

Who have their hands up?

Whose are the legs in the bottom right?

Who would the people in the top right be?

How does the cartoonist see Goering and Goebbels?

What does he mean by the caption?

5. This Allied cartoon had the caption *"Buck Benito rides again"*. Who is on the horse and what sort of horse is it? Why do you think it is tied to the tank? Whose tank is it?

What sort of commentary on Italo-German relations is it? What do you think Hitler and Mussolini would have thought of it? List any similarities you can see between what the cartoon is trying to say and the following comment made by Hitler in 1945.

> *. . . the Italian alliance rendered more service to the enemy than ourselves. . . . Her intervention in 1940 . . . had the sole effect of tarnishing our victory . . . we were prevented from following a revolutionary policy . . . by linking our fate with that of the Italians. . . . Italy's entry into the war gave our adversaries their first victories. . . .*

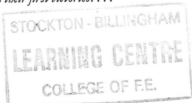
58

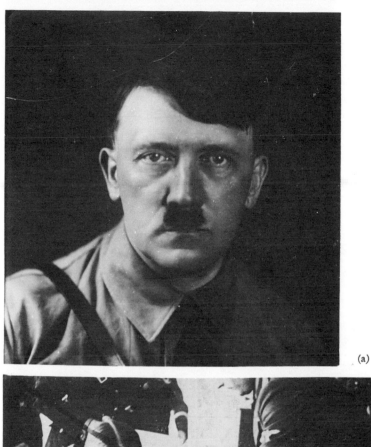

(a)

(b)

6. Look carefully at these two photographs. Why would Hitler want (a) to be published and (b) to be suppressed?

Goering handing out pin-up photos of Hitler to admiring girls.

Hitler surrounded by young Nazis.

7. The two photographs above were used for propaganda purposes. Why do you think they would be effective in the Nazi propaganda programme?

8. What propaganda purposes would be served by these photographs of Hitler and Mussolini?

Mussolini with his wife and family.

Hitler with young children.

Further Sources

Documentary Sources

Mussolini and the Fascist Era Desmond Gregory (THE ARCHIVE SERIES, EDWARD ARNOLD, 1968)
Hitler and the Rise of the Nazis D. M. Phillips (THE ARCHIVE SERIES, EDWARD ARNOLD, 1968)
The Nazi Years ed. Joachim Remak (PRENTICE-HALL, 1969)

Reference

Hitler, A Study in Tyranny Alan Bullock (PENGUIN, 1969)
Fascism in Western Europe 1900–45 H. R. Kedward (BLACKIE, 1969)

General Reading

Mussolini and Italy C. Bayne-Jardine (LONGMAN, 1966)
Hitler and Germany B. J. Elliot (LONGMAN, 1966)

Fiction

Two stories by Thomas Mann are of interest: *Disorder and Early Sorrow*, dealing with the problems of a family during the Weimar Inflation; and *Mario and the Magician*, set in Italy in the 1920s.